LAS VEGAS
and
LAUGHLIN, NEVADA

Automobile Club of Southern California

Cover photo courtesy of Las Vegas News Bureau.

Fireworks on Fremont Street

Writer... Sandy Schaack Brown
Graphic Artist .... Maria Morales-Gordon
Cartographer ....Donald Olivares

Editors ....Judy van Wingerden
Kristine Miller

Although information presented in this publication has been carefully researched and was as accurate as possible at press time, the Automobile Club of Southern California is not responsible for any changes or errors which may occur. It is wise to verify information immediately prior to your visit.

Only attractions or establishments that are approved by an Automobile Club of Southern California field representative may advertise. The purchase of advertising, however, has no effect on inspections and evaluations. Advertisements provide the reader with additional information which may be useful in selecting what to see and where to stay.

Additional advertisements (excluding attractions and establishments) for travel-related services may also be included in ACSC publications. Acceptance of these advertisements does not imply endorsement by ACSC.

AAA DISCOUNT

Certain attractions offer AAA and CAA members a special discount. The discount is given to both adults and children unless otherwise specified and applies to the member and his or her family traveling together, usually up to six persons. The discount may not apply if any other gate reduction is offered or if tickets are purchased through an agent rather than at the attraction's ticket office. The period of validity may vary from attraction to attraction. Be sure to ask if the discount is available at the time of your visit.

ISBN: 1-56413-187-4
Printed in the United States of America

GET EVERYTHING FOR YOUR TRIP. FREE.

Maps, TourBooks® & Area Guides

Fee-Free American Express® Travelers Cheques

AIRLINE TICKETS

Complete Airline & Travel Reservations

Car Rental Reservations & Discounts

Hotel/Motel Reservations & Discounts

Dependable Emergency Road Service

Join the Auto Club of Southern California today and we'll give you everything you need for your trip. ✦ Free maps ✦ Free TourBooks®, CampBooks® and area guides ✦ Fee-free American Express® Travelers Cheques and ✦ Free Triptiks®, a personalized, mile-by-mile routing of your entire trip. And you'll love saving money with Member-only discounts on ✦ Tours and cruises ✦ Hotel/motel reservations ✦ Rental cars and ✦ Popular attractions across the country. All of these great travel benefits can be yours for $38 a year plus a $20 enrollment fee -- a total of just $58. So why wait? Join AAA today and get everything for your trip. Free!

Call 1-800-882-5550, Ext. 149 (Outside So. CA: 1-800-AAA-HELP)

CONTENTS

KEY MAP 6
LAS VEGAS AND LAUGHLIN 7

LAS VEGAS

INTRODUCTION AND HISTORY 8
TRANSPORTATION 10
    Traveling to Las Vegas 10
    Local Transportation...13
CASINO GAMES 15
ENTERTAINMENT—MAIN SHOWROOMS............................... 17
SPORTS AND SPA FACILITIES 22
    Golf and Country Clubs 22
    Spa Facilities 25
    Swimming..25
    Tennis and Racquetball...26
SHOPPING... 28
MARRIAGE INFORMATION 30
ANNUAL EVENTS 32
LAS VEGAS AREA MAP... 34
LAS VEGAS STRIP MAP 36
DOWNTOWN AREA MAP..38
POINTS OF INTEREST 39
    Las Vegas..39
    Surrounding Areas 47
    Guided Tours 56
LAS VEGAS REGION MAP...60
ACTIVITIES FOR CHILDREN 62
CAMPING 65
    Las Vegas..66
    Surrounding Areas 69
LODGING AND RESTAURANTS..71

LAUGHLIN

INTRODUCTION AND HISTORY 92
TRANSPORTATION 94
    Traveling to Laughlin..94
    Local Transportation..95
CASINO GAMES 97
ENTERTAINMENT 99
SPORTS AND RECREATION 101
    Boating 101
    Fishing...101
    Golf..103
    Inner Tubing...103
    Swimming...103
    Tennis 104
    Waterskiing 104
ANNUAL EVENTS...105
LAUGHLIN-BULLHEAD CITY MAP 106
LAUGHLIN-LAKE HAVASU AREA MAP 107
POINTS OF INTEREST 108
    Guided Tours 112
ACTIVITIES FOR CHILDREN...114
CAMPING 116
LODGING AND RESTAURANTS 119
REFERENCE PHONE NUMBERS 124
    Las Vegas..124
    Laughlin 125
INDEX TO POINTS OF INTEREST 126
INDEX TO ADVERTISERS 128

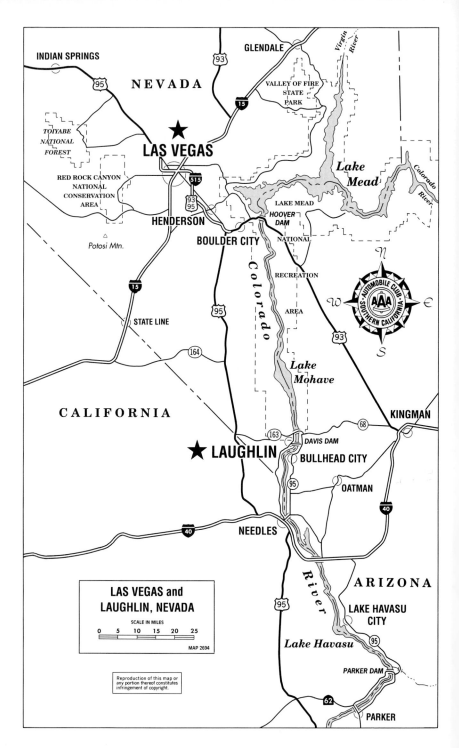

LAS VEGAS and
LAUGHLIN, NEVADA

SCALE IN MILES

0   5   10   15   20   25

MAP 2694

Reproduction of this map or
any portion thereof constitutes
infringement of copyright.

LAS VEGAS AND LAUGHLIN

Las Vegas and Laughlin, Nevada are both like shooting stars in the desert. Like a sparkling nebula in the empty darkness of nighttime, Las Vegas attracts more than 23 million visitors a year, making it one of the nation's favorite vacation destinations. About two hours to the south and on the banks of the Colorado River is Laughlin— a relatively new star of explosive growth, now the fourth largest gaming resort in the country.

*L*as Vegas has 30 years on Laughlin as a gambling mecca. It's a 24-hour city that sees most of its casino action at night, but it also offers resort and spa facilities, world-class golf courses, desert treks, shopping and other attractions in the daytime. Top-name entertainment, fancy accommodations at reasonable prices, all-you-can-eat buffets, miles of glittering neon, show girls in skimpy outfits—like the poker and slot tournaments and the casino come-ons, they all contribute to a vacation extravaganza the typical visitor finds hard to resist.

Laughlin is a haven for "snowbirds" in winter and an oasis for the sun-baked river crowd in summer. Besides gambling, what draws people to Laughlin are fishing, houseboating and waterskiing. Where Las Vegas is intense, Laughlin is more relaxed. In some ways they're alike, in others they're quite different. A visit to either of these celestial superstars can be like a ride on the tail of a comet.

The purpose of this book is to acquaint travelers with activities available in both these cities. Las Vegas is listed in the front of the book, Laughlin in the back. Each has accommodations at the end of its section. The *Contents* is useful for looking up categories such as "Casino Games" and "Shopping." The *Index* can be used to look up individual attractions or special tours. Detailed maps of both cities and their surrounding areas are included.

It's wise when planning a trip to either of these destinations to plan ahead and make reservations well in advance. Auto Club district offices in California and Nevada can assist Auto Club members with reservations for hotels, air travel and rental cars, as well as up-to-date mapping service, emergency road service information and a current list of shows and events in both cities.

LAS VEGAS
PAST

The modern history of Las Vegas began in 1855, when a small group of Mormon settlers arrived. They came to protect the mail route between Los Angeles and Salt Lake City, but for the next three years they were also engaged in fruit and vegetable cultivation and lead mining at Potosi Mountain. The Mormons abandoned their mining activity when the bullets made from their ore proved to be flaky and brittle, a problem that other miners would like to have had, since the lead ore had an extremely high silver content. Raids by the local Native Americans also added to their problems.

*A*fter the Mormons' departure in 1858, the area was left to the native tribes. In 1864 Nevada was admitted to the Union as the 36th state, although the 11,000 square miles surrounding Las Vegas were part of the Arizona territory. It was not until two years later that Congress ceded the region to Nevada, establishing the current borders.

Las Vegas News Bureau

Fremont Street (1929) as Las Vegas awaits inspection as a housing center for thousands of Boulder Dam (Hoover Dam) construction workers.

Las Vegas, Spanish for "The Meadows," developed gradually as a farming and ranching community. But in 1905 rapid growth started when the Union Pacific Railroad auctioned off 1200 lots in a single day, lots which soon began to sprout gambling houses, saloons and stores. The area continued its expansion for over 20 years, and then in 1928 Congress passed the Boulder Canyon Project Act. By 1931, construction on Hoover Dam had begun. Thousands of jobless men, victims of the nation's Great Depression, streamed into the Las Vegas-Boulder City area. At its peak, the Boulder Project employed more than 5000 men, with an average monthly payroll of $500,000. Coincidentally, 1931 was also the year that the Nevada Legislature legalized gambling in the state, though at the time the act was completely overshadowed by the attention being paid to the dam. In 1935 Franklin Roosevelt dedicated the structure, known then as "Boulder Dam." In April 1947, by congressional action, the 727-foot-high structure was officially designated Hoover Dam, the name by which it is known today.

The great hydroelectric project on the Colorado River originally brought power to Las Vegas, and this abundant source of electricity helped create the famous neon city. (Today Las Vegas' power primarily comes from coal burning power stations.) In 1940 a group of Los Angeles investors, speculating on the resort potential of the area, built El Rancho Vegas, the first hotel on what became the Las Vegas Strip. Shortly thereafter, the Last Frontier was completed, followed by the Fabulous Flamingo, a hotel and casino built by the infamous Bugsy Siegel. The momentum established by these early resorts continues to the present.

TODAY

Today Las Vegas is a highly developed resort in southern Nevada where legalized casino gambling and headline entertainment have combined to create the single most popular tourist destination in the United States. It accommodates, feeds and entertains more than 23 million visitors each year, a considerable accomplishment for a metropolitan area with a population of 900,000 permanent residents. Impressive statistics, however, do not explain the attraction. People come to Las Vegas for many different reasons, yet everyone seems to enjoy the vibrant pace and continuous activity.

TRANSPORTATION

Getting to Las Vegas is easy, and transportation choices abound. Most people take to the roads, but many others prefer to fly, or hop on a bus or train. Once in Las Vegas, visitors will find that the city's abundant taxis, buses, and trolleys are a convenient and inexpensive way to get around town.

TRAVELING TO LAS VEGAS

Air

Direct flights connect 11 cities in California with McCarran International Airport in Las Vegas. The connecting cities and carriers are shown below.

Auto

Las Vegas entertains millions of visitors each year, and not surprisingly more than half of them arrive by automobile. Nearly 4 million people a year drive to Nevada's largest city from the state of California. Southern Californians account for most of the automobile traffic. With the 65 mph speed limit in effect on I-15, Los Angeles is only about 5½ hours driving time from Las Vegas, and San Diego is about an hour farther. The San Francisco Bay Area is some 11 hours away by car, exclusive of stops. Although the 65 mph speed limit is

DIRECT FLIGHTS TO LAS VEGAS

FROM → VIA	AMERICAN	AMERICA WEST	DELTA	SOUTHWEST	UNITED	USAIR
BURBANK				●		
FRESNO			●			●
LOS ANGELES	●	●	●	●		
OAKLAND		●		●		
ONTARIO		●		●		
ORANGE COUNTY		●	●			
PALM SPRINGS			●			
SACRAMENTO		●		●		
SAN DIEGO		●		●		
SAN FRANCISCO		●			●	●
SAN JOSE				●		

For complete schedule information and help in arranging flights from cities with direct or connecting service, contact any Auto Club Travel Agency office, or phone the Club's Airline Express Desk. In Southern California call (800) 222-5000, Monday through Friday from 8 a.m. to 6 p.m.; in Northern California call (800) 352-1955, Monday through Friday 8:30 a.m. to 5:30 p.m.

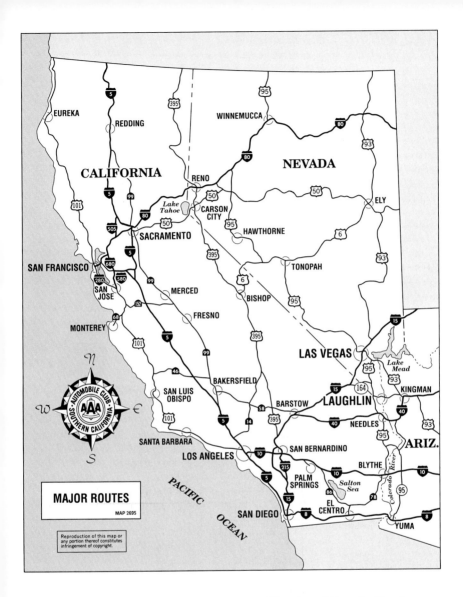

MAJOR ROUTES

MAP 2695

Reproduction of this map or any portion thereof constitutes infringement of copyright.

in effect for almost all of the driving along I-15 in both California and Nevada, weather and road conditions often dictate a lower speed. Drivers should also be alert to lower posted speed limits in populated areas.

Bus

Greyhound/Trailways offers service to Las Vegas from virtually any town in California and Nevada. No advance reservations are accepted, and tickets are usually purchased just prior to departure. For complete information, contact the ticket office in the nearest bus station. Greyhound/Trailways uses the bus terminal building on Main Street at Carson Avenue in downtown Las Vegas.

Desert Driving Hints

Regardless of your departure point, any automobile trip from California to Las Vegas will involve some desert driving. At all times, but especially during the summer months, take some basic precautions when crossing the Mojave Desert.

Make certain that the engine and cooling system of your car are in good working order, checking closely for radiator leaks, worn fan belts and cracked hoses. Tires should be properly inflated before starting out, but do not release air if they become overly hard while crossing the desert; stop the car and allow the tires to cool, then proceed. You should carry about five gallons of water in a clean container so that it can be used both for the radiator and for drinking. If the car overheats, do not remove the radiator cap immediately because of the risk of explosion. After the engine has cooled, slowly remove the cap and add water, leaving about an inch of air space between the water level and the top of the radiator. If an older model car experiences vapor lock, wrap a wet towel around the gas line between the fuel pump and the carburetor. This should cool the line and allow the car to start.

Keep an eye on the gasoline gauge and buy fuel when it is available; don't put yourself in the position of needing gasoline when you are on a stretch of highway between towns. Towns in the Mojave Desert are few and far between.

Desert driving often means that "out of the ordinary" precautions must be taken if your car becomes disabled. For instance, pulling the car as far off the road as possible is ordinarily the most desirable action to take, but in many areas the desert terrain does not offer a firm gravel surface off the asphalt shoulder. If you drive off the shoulder into soft sand, you may find yourself requiring a tow truck to get back onto the road. Once safely out of the traffic lane, activate your hazard warning lights. Do not abandon the car to go for help. It is often a long walk to the nearest town or even to a phone. High desert temperatures in summer months bring a real threat of heat stroke, and even a short walk could become dangerous. Normal procedures can be followed when weather permits: remain in your car, keep your seat belt fastened, headrest properly positioned, doors locked and wait for assistance. In extreme desert heat this will not be possible. Even with the windows rolled down, the car will become unbearably hot. Seek out a shady area to wait for assistance, either in the shadow of the vehicle itself or in the shade of nearby vegetation. Do not leave pets or children in the car—they suffer the effects of the heat even more quickly than adults.

The best course of action the Auto Club can recommend is to wait for assistance from the Highway Patrol. Highway Patrol officers routinely make regular patrols of desert highways and will offer aid and assistance. We advise extreme caution in accepting help from anyone you do not know.

Rental Cars

Auto Club Travel Agency offices and the Airline Express Desk can also help you secure a rental car reservation in advance of your trip. Rental cars are available on a daily, weekly and monthly basis from nationally known and local car-leasing agencies. In Las Vegas many of the firms have offices at McCarran International Airport and along the Strip. Check the telephone directory yellow pages under "Automobile Renting and Leasing."

For tourists who come to Las Vegas via public transportation and plan to sightsee, a rental car could be a desirable alternative to tours, buses and cabs. You have the advantage of not being confined to a schedule, and for families or groups of three or more, the shared cost of a rental car could be less than the combined charges for tours and taxis.

The Hertz rental car agency offers discounts to AAA members at participating locations; call (800) 654-3080.

Train

Amtrak's "Desert Wind" provides daily service between Los Angeles and Las Vegas. The train originates at Union Passenger Terminal in Los Angeles and stops to take on and discharge passengers in Fullerton, San Bernardino, Victorville and Barstow. The Amtrak station in Las Vegas is located downtown at The Union Plaza Hotel. Total traveling time from Los Angeles to Las Vegas is seven hours. Auto Club Travel Agency offices and the Airline Express Desk can also help you with Amtrak reservations prior to your trip.

LOCAL TRANSPORTATION

The **Downtown Transportation Center**, located at Stewart Avenue and Casino Center Boulevard, serves as a transportation hub for Citizens Area Transit buses and the downtown trolley. Most bus lines connect to the center, as does the trolley system. The center is open daily from 6 a.m. to 10 p.m. and has a restaurant, as well as ticket and route information personnel.

Bus

One easy way to travel from place to place on the Strip, or between the Strip and downtown, is to take the Citizens Area Transit (CAT) bus that operates between Vacation Village at the southernmost end of the Strip and the downtown area. CAT uses a grid-type bus system that makes traveling convenient.

Seven days a week, from 5 a.m. to midnight, the CAT bus (Route 301) runs at 10 minute intervals north and south along the Strip between the southernmost point, Vacation Village, and the northernmost point, the Downtown Transportation Center. From midnight to 5 a.m., the bus takes the same route but at 15 minute intervals.

The CAT bus (Route 302) runs at 30 minute intervals from 5:45 a.m. to 1:15 a.m. from McCarran International Airport, north along Swenson to the Strip at St. Louis and south along the Strip to Vacation Village. Northbound, the bus operates from 5:30 a.m. to 1 a.m., starting at Vacation Village, north along the Strip to St. Louis, south on Paradise to McCarran Airport.

The one-way fare is $1; senior citizens 65 and over, youths ages 5-17 and persons with disabilities 50¢. Free for children under age 5. Exact change is required. Tokens (called CAT Coins) or a monthly pass can be purchased at the Downtown Transportation Center.

Local residential bus service to several areas, including Henderson and Boulder City, is also available. For more information call (702) CAT-RIDE.

Downtown Trolley

Shuttle buses designed to look like trolleys depart the Downtown Transportation Center daily every 20 minutes from 7:30 a.m. to 11 p.m. The route traveled is along Ogden Avenue (eastbound) to the Charleston Plaza Shopping Center and Fremont Street (westbound) between Main and 15th streets. The entire route takes 40 minutes to travel. Fares are 50¢ for adults, 25¢ for seniors, persons with disabilities and those under 17. For information call (702) 229-6024. (Do not confuse this trolley with the Strip trolley—they do not connect.) See *Downtown* map.

Trolley service to Meadows Mall is also provided nine times a day from 10:30 a.m. to 5 p.m. Monday through Saturday. There is no Sunday or holiday service. The fare is $1.10 for adults, 55¢ for seniors, persons with disabilities and those under 17. For information call (702) 229-6024.

Strip Trolley

Like the downtown trolley, the Strip trolley also uses shuttle buses designed to look like trolleys. The trolleys operate daily from 9:30 a.m. to 2 a.m. along Las Vegas Boulevard South from the Hacienda Resort Hotel on the south end to the Sahara Hotel on the north end. An additional loop includes the Las Vegas Hilton Hotel and a portion of Paradise Road. The trolleys pass by each stop approximately every 30 minutes.

The fare is $1. For more information call (702) 382-1404. (Do not confuse this trolley with the downtown trolley—their routes do not connect.) See *Strip* map.

Taxi

For visitors who come to Las Vegas to enjoy gaming and entertainment, a trouble-free and economical way of getting around is by cab. The base fare is $2.20 for the first one-seventh mile and $1.40 for each additional mile. There is also a $1.20 tax per load for pickups at McCarran International Airport. Taxis are plentiful, particularly at the entrances of the major resort hotels, and by using them you avoid the nuisance of having to find a parking space in a crowded lot or the tip for valet service. In addition, if two or three people are sharing one taxi, it compares favorably to the cost of the bus, and there is usually no waiting. A typical trip half the length of the Strip will cost about $6-$9; a trip from the middle of the Strip to the airport will cost about $11.

If you are staying at a hotel or motel which is not frequented by cabs or wish to arrange for a taxi at a particular time, you can phone any of the following companies for service in Las Vegas. Upon request, ABC Union, Ace, ANLV and Vegas Western provide vans with wheelchair lifts at regular taxi rates.

ABC Union....................(702) 736-8444
Ace ....(702) 736-8383
ANLV...........................(702) 643-1041
Checker/Star/Yellow ..(702) 873-2000
Desert ....(702) 376-2688
Nellis............................(702) 252-0201
Vegas Western.............(702) 736-6121
Whittlesea Blue............(702) 384-6111

CASINO GAMES

Beautiful resorts, headline entertainers, championship golf courses, swimming pools and tennis courts—all of these attractions bring people to Las Vegas. But without legalized gambling, the scale of this desert development would be considerably smaller. From 1931 until the mid-1970s, Nevada was the only state that had casino gaming. This helped to make Las Vegas the single most popular tourist destination in the United States. Today more than 23 million visitors a year pour into the city. The profits from gambling are enormous, and most efforts to attract new visitors could not be underwritten without the lucrative casinos.

*I*f you are inclined toward trying one or more of the many games of chance, be sure to familiarize yourself with the rules and strategy of the games before taking the plunge. Most of the large resort hotels offer gambling instruction in their casinos and, in some cases, on the hotel's cable television channel. Not only will you increase the odds of winning, you will also enjoy playing more if you understand some of the intricacies of the games. Do not expect dealers or croupiers to be of much help; they have a job to do and will offer assistance and advice only when they can. If the games are completely new to you, watch the action for a while before joining in; observation is a cheap way of learning some of the more obvious lessons.

If you have had some experience gambling but wish to better your skills, read one or two of the books devoted to casino gambling. They have a complete explanation of the rules, strategy, odds, wagering and systems which claim to give you the advantage. But be skeptical of the systems: statistically they might work in the long run,

but few players have the time and the resources to last, or the concentration and mental dexterity that they often require. The serious student will spend some time practicing at home before venturing into the casino to test his or her mettle. And finally, decide how much you can afford to lose and put that money aside. Should it cross to the other side of the tables, don't dig into your pockets for more— it is not just a cliché that people can lose everything they have.

Baccarat: A game very similar to chemin de fer, baccarat is played with six decks of cards dealt from a box called a "shoe." Two cards are given to each of two players, with one player being designated the bank. The object is to get a hand totaling nine, with all tens and face cards counted as zero. Other people at the table bet on either the bank or the player. Baccarat is usually a high-stakes game associated with the glamour crowd.

Bingo: Most bingo games in Las Vegas are played on "boards" with three bingo cards on each board. There is both open-play and party bingo at most casinos. In open-play bingo, each board costs between 10 and 40 cents per game. Party bingo is played at set hours; cards cost $1 to $4 each with a $3 to $6 minimum; approximately 10 to 12 games are played during each party session.

Blackjack: Sometimes called "21," blackjack is a popular card game where up to seven people play individually against a dealer. Deceptively simple, the object of the game is to beat the dealer by getting as close to 21 as possible without going over that count.

Craps: By far the most complicated casino game, craps offers literally dozens of different ways to bet on the dice. The action is fast and the amount of money exchanging hands is considerable. Craps is not a good game for the timid, but it's great fun to watch.

Keno: This is an adaptation of an ancient Chinese game which has the advantage of allowing the player to risk a small amount of money, roughly a dollar, for a possible $50,000 return. Out of a possible 80 numbers, 20 are drawn at random; if your numbers come up, you win.

Poker: The rules are pretty much the same for casino poker as they are for home games, except that the house provides a dealer who manages the game without playing a hand. The house makes money by taking a small percentage of each pot. Check the rules carefully before sitting down at a game.

Roulette: There are 38 numbers on a roulette wheel, and you can bet on one of them, a group, a color or a column. You don't have to worry about skill because the game is strictly one for luck and intuition. Low stake games are common, so a few dollars can keep you going for quite a while.

Slot Machines: Many people come to Las Vegas to play the one-armed bandits. There are nickel, dime, quarter, half-dollar, dollar, 5-, 25-, 100- and 500-dollar machines—the more you risk, the more you can win, and not coincidentally, the more you can lose.

Race and Sports Books: You can bet on practically any horse race, boxing match, or professional or collegiate game (as long as it does not involve a Nevada event). You can find this kind of action in the casinos and in separate betting parlors. Most of the major hotels have race and sports books.

ENTERTAINMENT— MAIN SHOWROOMS

Headline entertainment is second only to gambling in the number of visitors it attracts to Las Vegas. The big showrooms feature either a well-known singer or comedian backed by an opening act, or a spectacular production with a large cast, elaborate sets and ornate costumes. In any case, the shows run about 90 minutes. For a current, two-month entertainment schedule, see the Auto Club's Las Vegas Shows schedule, available at all Auto Club district offices.

A list of the major showrooms in Las Vegas follows. Please note that prices given are per-person minimums and usually do not include the 7 percent sales tax, 10 percent entertainment tax or any gratuities. In addition to these extra charges, minimums will often be raised for some especially popular entertainers, as well as for opening and closing nights.

Although the early and late shows are basically the same in terms of content, children are not admitted to the late shows. The hour alone prevents most children from enjoying themselves, and entertainers like to feel freer to use language and discuss subjects that might not be appropriate for a general audience. For this reason, not only children but sensitive adults should attend the early shows. Production shows with nude performers usually do not admit children.

Many showrooms now offer advance ticket sales and in some cases, reserved seating. Tickets can be purchased one to four weeks in advance at the showroom ticket office or through a local ticket agency. There are a number of ticket agencies in Las Vegas which specialize in booking entertainment. You will find them listed in the telephone directory yellow pages under "Theatre and Sports Ticket Service" or "Tourist Information."

In some cases, tickets admit you only to the room and do not guarantee any particular seat. A line to enter the showroom will begin forming 60 to 90 minutes prior to showtime. Seating is first come, first served, except for a small number of seats reserved for special casino customers. Those with tickets to shows that have assigned seats need only arrive 15 to 30 minutes prior to showtime.

When going to a dinner show, remember that the time given is performance time. You should arrive at the theater about two hours early for a dinner performance.

Often large production shows run indefinitely, many of them for several years. Those shows scheduled to run indefinitely, as of press time, appear in the listings, but any show is subject to change without notice. Visitors are advised to verify shows, times and prices in advance.

Aladdin Hotel, 3667 Las Vegas Blvd. S., (702) 736-0240
Aladdin Showroom — "Country Tonite" (Indefinitely)
700 seats
7:15 and 10 p.m. (cocktails)
$21.95 (buffet)
$17.95 (cocktails)
Ages 18 and under $14.95 (buffet); $11.95 (show only)
Tickets also sold through Ticketmaster
Dark Tuesday

Bally's Casino Resort, 3645 Las Vegas Blvd. S., (702) 739-4567
Celebrity Room — Top-name entertainment
1450 seats
One show nightly (cocktails)
Prices vary with entertainers

Jubilee Theatre — "Jubilee" (Indefinitely)
1050 seats
8 p.m. only, Monday and Tuesday
8 and 11 p.m., Wednesday, Thursday and Saturday
4 and 7:30 p.m., Sunday
$40 minimum
Must be 18 years of age to attend
Dark Friday

Caesars Palace, 3570 Las Vegas Blvd. S., (702) 731-7333
Circus Maximus — Top-name entertainment
1126 seats
Times and prices vary with entertainers
Cocktails available a la carte
Tickets on sale 30 days in advance

Excalibur Hotel/Casino, 3850 Las Vegas Blvd. S.,
(800) 937-7777; (702) 597-7600
King Arthur's Arena — "King Arthur's Tournament" (Indefinitely)
925 seats
6 and 8:30 p.m. (dinner)
$24.95 minimum
Tickets available six days prior to performance

Flamingo Hilton Hotel, 3555 Las Vegas Blvd. S.,
(702) 733-3111; (702) 733-3333
Flamingo Showroom — "City Lites" (Indefinitely)
750 seats
7:45 p.m. (dinner)
11 p.m. (cocktails)
$28.50 minimum (dinner); $20.95 minimum (cocktails)
Dark Sunday

Elaborate stage productions such as "City Lites" entertain thousands of visitors with dazzling sets and beautiful dancers.

Hacienda Resort Hotel, 3950 Las Vegas Blvd. S., (702) 739-8911
   Fiesta Theatre — "Lance Burton—A Magical Journey" (Indefinitely)
      550 seats
      8 and 11 p.m.
      $19.95 minimum
      Reservations available day of performance
      Dark Monday

Harrah's-Las Vegas, 3475 Las Vegas Blvd. S., (702) 369-5222
   Commander's Theatre — "Spellbound—A Concert of Illusion"
(Indefinitely)
      525 seats
      7:30 and 10 p.m. (cocktails)
      $21.95 minimum (includes one drink)
      Reserved seats
      Dark Sunday

Imperial Palace, 3535 Las Vegas Blvd. S., (702) 794-3261
   Imperial Theatre — "Legends in Concert" (Indefinitely)
      843 seats
      7:30 and 10:30 p.m. (cocktails)
      $23.50 minimum (includes two drinks)
      Children 12 and under $11.75
      Dark Sunday, except holidays

Las Vegas Hilton, 3000 Paradise Rd., (702) 732-5755; (800) STARLIGHT
   Hilton Showroom — Andrew Lloyd Webber's "Starlight Express"
   (Indefinitely)
      1450 seats
      7:30 and 10:30 p.m.,Tuesday and Friday through Sunday
      9 p.m., Wednesday and Thursday
      $39.50 minimum
      Children 12 and under $25
      Tickets available two months in advance
      Dark Monday

Luxor, 3900 Las Vegas Blvd. S., (702) 262-4900
   Pharaoh's Theatre — "Winds of the Gods" (Indefinitely)
      1120 seats
      7:30 and 10:15 p.m. (cocktails)
      $19.95 minimum
      Dark Sunday

MGM Grand Hotel Casino and Theme Park, 3799 Las Vegas Blvd. S.,
   (702) 891-7777
   *Show information was not available at press time. Call the hotel for
   information.*

The Mirage, 3400 Las Vegas Blvd. S., (702) 791-7111; (702) 792-7777
   Theatre Mirage — "Siegfried and Roy at the Mirage" (Indefinitely)
      1500 seats
      7:30 and 11 p.m. (cocktails)
      $72.85 (includes two drinks and souvenir program)
      Tickets available three days in advance
      Dark Wednesday

Riviera Hotel, 2901 Las Vegas Blvd. S.
   Versailles Theatre — (702) 794-9301
   "Splash" (Indefinitely)
      850 seats
      7:30 and 10:30 p.m. (cocktails)
      $32.18 minimum (includes two drinks)
      Children 5-12, $29.18

   Mardi Gras Entertainment Center — (702) 794-9300
   "Crazy Girls—Sensuality and Passion" (Indefinitely)
      550 seats
      8:30 and 11 p.m.
      $15.46 (includes two drinks); $21.75 (buffet)
      Dark Monday

   "An Evening at La Cage" (Indefinitely)
      625 seats
      7, 9 and 11 p.m.
      $16.95 (includes two drinks); $24.90 (buffet)
      Dark Tuesday

Sahara Hotel, 2535 Las Vegas Blvd. S., (702) 737-2515
Congo Room — "Boy-lesque" (Indefinitely)
    600 seats
    8 and midnight Thursday through Tuesday
    $17.50 minimum
    Dark Wednesday

"The Rich Little Show" (Indefinitely)
    10 p.m. Friday through Wednesday
    $24.50 minimum
    Dark Thursday

Sheraton Desert Inn, 3145 Las Vegas Blvd. S., (702) 733-4566
Crystal Room — Top-name entertainment
    636 seats
    9 p.m. Tuesday through Sunday
    Prices vary with entertainers
    Dark Monday

Stardust Hotel, 3000 Las Vegas Blvd. S., (800) 824-6033; (702) 732-6325
Stardust Theatre — "Enter the Night" (Indefinitely)
    850 seats
    8 and 11 p.m. Wednesday through Saturday (cocktails)
    9 p.m. Sunday and Monday (cocktails)
    $24.90 minimum (includes two drinks)
    Dark Tuesday

Treasure Island, 3300 Las Vegas Blvd. S., (702) 894-7722
Treasure Island Showroom — "Le Cirque du Soleil—Mystère"
(Indefinitely)
    1500 seats
    7:30 and 10:30 p.m. nightly
    $42 minimum
    Children 12 and under, $21
    Dark Monday

Tropicana Resort and Casino, 3801 Las Vegas Blvd. S., (702) 739-2411
Tiffany Theatre — "Folies Bergere" (Indefinitely)
    1050 seats
    7:30 p.m. (dinner)
    10:30 p.m. (cocktails)
    $26.95 (dinner); $19.95 (includes two drinks)
    Dark Thursday

SPORTS AND SPA FACILITIES

With an average of 310 sunny days a year, Las Vegas is an ideal spot for outdoor recreation sports. Not only are there acres of lush green golf courses and more than 85 tennis courts, but there are swimming pools at all the major hotels and motels, amusement parks, water rides, and so much more. And after a hard day of having fun, visitors can rejuvenate in the luxurious spas and health clubs located in the city's major hotels.

GOLF AND COUNTRY CLUBS

Golf is one of the principal outdoor attractions in Las Vegas. There are a number of championship courses, some of which host PGA and LPGA tournaments, and several less demanding courses where the weekend golfer can enjoy a quick round. The desert climate offers nearly ideal playing conditions all year, with the exception of very high midday temperatures in July and August. In summer, golfers should arrange an early starting time to avoid the extreme heat.

Public, semi-private and private courses are listed by community within the book's two designated areas. Each golf course listing gives general street directions from the nearest freeway. For detailed directions refer to Automobile Club of Southern California street maps.

Information given for each course includes name, location, mailing address, phone number and facilities, plus yardage, par and slope and USGA ratings (all from men's white tees). Some 9-hole courses show a slope and USGA rating that reflects play on that 9 holes plus another 9-hole course, or double play on the same course. Unless otherwise stated, each course is open daily all year. The abbreviation N/A means the information was not available. Package plan indicates a special rate combining hotel or resort rooms and golfing fees. Greens fees are given for weekday and weekend play during peak season. Many 9-hole courses list 18-hole fees because they require 18 holes of play. Some courses have senior citizen rates. Military golf courses listed in this publication show greens fees that apply to civilian guests of military personnel.

Information in this book is published as it is received from the individual courses. The publication has been made as complete as possible; a few courses, however, have been intentionally omitted at the request of the owners.

All semi-private and private courses have restrictions on public play ranging from members and guests only to liberal reciprocal agreements with members of other courses. It is impossible to list all of the restrictions for each course, so please telephone the course directly if in doubt. Reservations are advised at most courses; some country clubs require reservations months in advance.

Boulder City

Boulder City Golf Course (Public)
(702) 293-9236
South of US 93 at 1 Clubhouse Dr, 89005. The course is 18 holes; 6132 yards; par 72; 103 slope; 68 rating. Rates: $17 weekdays and weekends. Clubhouse, golf shop, professional, power and hand carts, rental clubs, driving range; restaurant, coffee shop, snack bar, cocktails.

Henderson

Black Mountain Golf & Country Club (Semi-private)
(702) 565-7933
10 mi se of Las Vegas via US 95 at 500 Greenway Rd; Box 91566, 89009. Closed Dec 25. The course is 18 holes; 6223 yards; par 72; 120 slope; 69.8 rating. Rates: $25 weekdays, $30 weekends. Clubhouse, locker room, golf shop, professional, power and hand carts, rental clubs, driving range; restaurant, coffee shop, snack bar, cocktails.

The Legacy Golf Club (Public)
(702) 897-2187
Intersection of Green Valley Pkwy and Wigwam at 130 Par Excellence Dr, 89014. Closed Dec 25. The course is 18 holes; 6211 yards; par 72; 118 slope; 69.1 rating. Rates: $85-$90 (mandatory golf cart included) weekdays and weekends. Clubhouse, golf shop, professional, power carts, rental clubs, driving range; restaurant, snack bar, cocktails.

Royal Kenfield Country Club (Public)
(702) 434-9009
8 mi se of Las Vegas at 1 Showboat Country Club Dr, 89014. The course is 18 holes; 5954 yards; par 72; 124 slope; 69.7 rating. Rates: $75 (mandatory golf cart included) weekdays and weekends. Golf shop, professional, power carts, rental clubs, driving range; snack bar, cocktails, beer, wine.

Las Vegas

Angel Park Golf Club (Public)
(702) 254-4653
West off SR 95 at Rainbow Blvd/Westcliff Dr at 100 S Rampart Blvd, 89128. The Mountain course is 18 holes; 5751 yards; par 71; 116 slope; 67.8 rating. Rates: $72 (mandatory golf cart included) weekdays and weekends. The Palm course is 18 holes; 5634 yards; par 71; 114 slope; 66.7 rating. Rates: $78 (mandatory golf cart included) weekdays and weekends. Clubhouse, locker room, golf shop, professional, power carts, rental clubs, lighted driving range; restaurant, snack bar, cocktails.

Craig Ranch Golf Course (Public)
(702) 642-9700
3 mi n off I-15 at 628 W Craig Rd, 89030. The course is 18 holes; 6001 yards; par 70; 105 slope; 66.8 rating. Rates: $13 weekdays and weekends. Clubhouse, golf shop, professional, power and hand carts, rental clubs, driving range; snack bar, beer, wine.

Desert Inn Country Club (Public)
(702) 733-4290
¾ mi e of I-15 off Flamingo Rd at 3145 Las Vegas Blvd S, 89109. Package plan. The course is 18 holes; 6581 yards; par 72; 129 slope; 72 rating. Rates: $150 (mandatory golf cart included) weekdays and weekends. Clubhouse, locker room, golf shop, professional, power carts, rental clubs, driving range; tennis, swimming; restaurant, coffee shop, snack bar, cocktails.

Desert Rose Golf Course (Public)

(702) 431-4653

6 mi e of I-15 off Sahara Ave at 5483 Clubhouse Dr, 89122. The course is 18 holes; 6135 yards; par 71; 108 slope; 68.7 rating. Rates: $37 weekdays, $39 weekends. Clubhouse, golf shop, professional, power and hand carts, rental clubs, driving range; restaurant, coffee shop, snack bar, cocktails.

Las Vegas Golf Club (Public)

(702) 646-3003

1½ mi n of US 95 via Decatur Blvd and Washington Ave at 4349 Vegas Dr, 89108. The course is 18 holes; 6337 yards; par 72; 114 slope; 70.3 rating. Rates: $12 weekdays and weekends. Clubhouse, golf shop, professional, power and hand carts, rental clubs, lighted driving range; restaurant, coffee shop, snack bar, cocktails.

Los Prados Country Club (Public)

(702) 645-5696

8 mi nw of US 95 via Lone Mountain Rd and Los Prados Blvd at 5150 Los Prados Circle, 89130. Closed Dec 25. The course is 18 holes; 5348 yards; par 70; 107 slope; 65.8 rating. Rates: $15 weekdays, $20 weekends. Clubhouse, locker room, golf shop, professional, power and hand carts, rental clubs; restaurant, snack bar, cocktails.

North Las Vegas Golf Course (Public)

(702) 649-7171

1 mi w of I-15 off Cheyenne Ave at 324 E Brooks Ave, 89036. The course is 9 holes; 1128 yards; par 27; N/A slope; N/A rating. Rates: $4 weekdays, $5 weekends. Clubhouse, golf shop, hand carts, rental clubs, lighted course; coffee shop, snack bar, beer.

Painted Desert Golf Course (Public)

(702) 645-2568

8½ mi nw off US 95 and Ann Rd at 5555 Painted Mirage Rd, 89110. The course is 18 holes; 6323 yards; par 72; 128 slope; 71 rating. Rates: $60 (mandatory golf cart included) weekdays and weekends. Clubhouse, golf shop, professional, power carts, rental clubs, driving range; snack bar, cocktails.

Sahara Country Club (Public)

(702) 796-0016

3 mi e of I-15 at 1911 E Desert Inn Rd, 89109. The course is 18 holes; 6418 yards; par 71; 119 slope; 71.1 rating. Rates: $80 (mandatory golf cart included) Mon-Thu; $85 (mandatory golf cart included) Fri-Sun. Clubhouse, golf shop, professional, power carts, rental clubs, lighted driving range; restaurant, snack bar, cocktails.

Spanish Trail Country Club (Private)

(702) 364-0357

4 mi w of I-15 off W Tropicana Ave at 5050 Spanish Trail Ln, 89113. Closed Dec 25. The Canyon course is 9 holes; 3306 yards; par 36; N/A slope; N/A rating. The Lakes course is 9 holes; 3210 yards; par 36; N/A slope; N/A rating. The Sunrise course is 9 holes; 3173 yards; par 36; N/A slope; N/A rating. Rates: N/A. Clubhouse, locker room, golf shop, professional, power carts, rental clubs, driving range; tennis, swimming; restaurant, coffee shop, snack bar, cocktails.

Sun City Summerlin Golf Club (Semi-private)

(702) 363-4373

10 mi nw off US 95 and Lake Mead Blvd at 9201-B Del Webb Blvd, 89128. Closed Dec 25. The

Highland Falls course is 18 holes; 6017 yards; par 72; N/A slope; N/A rating. The Palm Valley course is 18 holes; 6341 yards; par 72; 124 slope; 69.8 rating. Rates: $75 (mandatory golf cart included) weekdays and weekends. Clubhouse, golf shop, professional, power carts, rental clubs, driving range; coffee shop, snack bar.

Sunrise Golf Club (Private)
(702) 456-3160
5 mi e of the Strip at 5500 E Flamingo Rd, 89122. Closed Dec 25. The North course is 18 holes; 6403 yards; par 72; 106 slope; 67.3 rating. The South course is 18 holes; 6547 yards; par 72; 115 slope; 70.7 rating. Rates: $40 weekdays, $70 (mandatory golf cart included) weekends. Clubhouse, locker room, golf shop, professional, power carts, rental clubs, driving range; restaurant, coffee shop, snack bar, cocktails.

Sunrise Vista (Private)
(702) 652-2602
10 mi e of Las Vegas at 2841 Kinley Dr, Nellis Air Force Base, 89191. Closed Jan 1, Thanksgiving and Dec 25. The course is 18 holes; 6463 yards; par 72; 116 slope; 70.4 rating. Rates: $18 weekdays and weekends. Clubhouse, locker room, golf shop, professional, power and hand carts, rental clubs, lighted driving range, snack bar, beer, wine.

NOTE: Canyon Gate Golf Course and Las Vegas Country Club requested not to have detailed listings.

SPA FACILITIES

Many hotels in Las Vegas have not only swimming pools, but also whirlpool, sauna, massage, exercise, spa or health club facilities.

Use of some facilities and services is free, while others like massage, steam room, spa and health club privileges often carry a fee. Policies vary at each establishment. A list of facilities and whether a fee is charged is included in the listing for each hotel in the accommodations section of the book. Spa or health club facilities are available at the following hotels:

Alexis Park Resort Hotel
Bally's Las Vegas
Caesars Palace
Flamingo Hilton
Golden Nugget Hotel
Harrah's-Las Vegas
Las Vegas Hilton
Luxor
MGM Grand
Mirage
Riviera Hotel
Sheraton Desert Inn
Treasure Island
Tropicana

The Sheraton Desert Inn and The Union Plaza hotels have jogging tracks.

Some of these health clubs admit only hotel guests. For a listing of public health clubs, check the yellow pages of the telephone directory.

SWIMMING

Although most visitors to Las Vegas will find that their accommodations include a swimming pool, there are a number of swimming pools in public parks which anyone can use. Pools are open daily 1 to 6 p.m. from early June to Labor Day. Fees are $1.25 for adults and 75¢ for ages 8 to 17; under 8, 50¢. For further information, call the Clark County Parks & Recreation Department at (702) 455-8200.

TENNIS AND RACQUETBALL

Many of the resort hotels in Las Vegas, as well as some private clubs, have tennis and racquetball courts. The resorts often give priority to their guests, restricting other visitors to open courts.
It is always a good idea to phone ahead, since hours and regulations governing play are subject to change.

PRIVATE
(Open only to guests of the hotel)

Las Vegas Hilton
(702) 732-5111
3000 Paradise Rd, 89193
6 outdoor courts; lighted. Reservations are necessary for play between 9 a.m. and 4 p.m.; open court play before or after. No fees.

Riviera Hotel
(702) 734-5110
2901 Las Vegas Blvd S, 89109
2 courts; lighted.
No fees.

SEMI-PRIVATE
(Open to the public)

Alexis Park Resort Hotel
(702) 796-3300; (800) 582-2228
375 E Harmon Ave, 89109
2 outdoor courts; lighted.
Priority to hotel guests.
No fees.

Bally's Las Vegas
(702) 739-4598
3645 Las Vegas Blvd S, 89109
10 outdoor courts; 5 lighted. Reservations are necessary for play between 8 a.m. and 8 p.m. Fees are $10 per hour for hotel guests; $15 per hour for visitors.

Caesars Palace
(702) 731-7786
3570 Las Vegas Blvd S, 89109
5 outdoor courts. Fees are $15 per hour for hotel guests; $25 per hour for visitors.

Flamingo Hilton
(702) 733-3344
3555 Las Vegas Blvd S, 89109
4 outdoor courts; lighted. Fees are $5 per hour for hotel guests; $12 per hour for visitors.

Las Vegas Athletic Club East
(702) 733-1919
1070 E Sahara Ave, 89104
8 racquetball courts. Reservations available. Fee is $10 for guest pass. Open 24 hours.

Las Vegas Athletic Club West
(702) 362-3720
3315 Spring Mountain Rd, 89103
8 racquetball courts. Reservations available. Fee is $10 for guest pass.

Las Vegas Sporting House
(702) 733-8999
3025 Industrial Rd, 89109
10 racquetball courts; 2 squash courts; 2 outdoor tennis courts; lighted. Discounts available for hotel guests. Fee is $20, and includes all facilities.

Sheraton Desert Inn
(702) 733-4577
3145 Las Vegas Blvd S, 89109
10 outdoor courts, 5 lighted. Reservations available. Free for hotel guests; $10 daily pass for visitors.

The Union Plaza Hotel
(702) 386-2275
1 Main St. 89101
4 outdoor courts; lighted.
Hotel guests have priority.

University of Nevada, Las Vegas

(702) 895-3150

On campus, near Harmon Ave and Swenson St.

12 outdoor tennis courts; lighted. 8 indoor racquetball courts. Reservations advised. Hours for tennis are 8 a.m. to 10 p.m. Racquetball courts open 6 a.m. to 10 p.m. Monday through Friday, 8 a.m. to 6 p.m. Saturday, and 10 a.m. to 6 p.m. Sunday. $2 guest fee.

PUBLIC

A number of publicly maintained tennis courts are located in Las Vegas. Courts are open daily from 6 a.m. to 11 p.m. and are open to anyone who wishes to use them. In the summer most people play during the cool morning hours and then again in the evening, so vacant courts are usually more difficult to find during these busy hours. Otherwise, there is rarely any problem in finding an empty court. Reservations may be made for a nominal fee, but are not required. For information or reservations, call Sunset Park at (702) 455-8200.

Cannon Junior High School,

5850 Euclid Ave.

3 outdoor courts; not lighted. Monday through Friday (after 5 p.m. when school is in session).

East Las Vegas Park & Recreation Center,

5700 East Missouri Ave.

3 outdoor courts; lighted.

Laurelwood Park,

4300 Newcastle Rd.

2 outdoor courts; lighted

Orr Junior High School,

1562 East Katie Ave.

4 outdoor courts; not lighted. Monday through Friday (after 5 p.m. when school is in session).

Paradise Park Recreation Center,

4770 South Harrison Dr.

2 outdoor courts; lighted.

Paul Meyer Park,

4525 New Forest Dr.

2 outdoor courts; lighted.

Sunset Park,

2575 East Sunset Dr.

8 outdoor courts; lighted. Reservations required. Frisbee golf course.

Winterwood Park,

5310 Consul Ave.

2 outdoor courts; lighted.

Woodbury Junior High School,

3875 East Harmon Ave.

3 courts. Monday through Friday.

SHOPPING

From small, unimposing souvenir shops and factory outlets to flashy indoor malls with upscale merchandise and talking statues, visitors will find that Las Vegas has a lot more going for it than gambling-it's a shoppers dream.

V isitors will have no trouble finding a gift shop in their hotel for replacing forgotten toothbrushes and for buying the latest magazines, newspapers, postcards, keychains, T-shirts, stuffed toys and other souvenir items with "Las Vegas" emblazoned on them. The gift shops are usually centrally located near the front entrance of the hotel, near the registration desk or the casino. It is also the most likely place for finding a U.S. Postal Service stamp machine.

For the real souvenir hound there is no shortage of trinket shops along the Strip area of Las Vegas Boulevard from Charleston Boulevard south to Tropicana Avenue. They have it all— hats, shirts, coffee mugs, salt and pepper shakers, genuine leather purses, wallets, toy guns, Indian dolls, turquoise jewelry, pens, promotional books, dice, cards, poker chips and back scratchers. Downtown these stores are usually located one block off Fremont Street between Main and 4th streets.

Some of the largest resort hotels have shopping arcades. These usually feature a dozen shops selling designer fashions, furs, jewelry, artworks, toys and international gifts. One of the largest of these arcades is Bally's Casino Resort-Las Vegas' 40-store shopping area. Sam's Town features a western-wear emporium, and its 40,000 square feet of retail space makes it one of the largest such stores west of the Rockies.

Boulevard Mall, *Maryland Parkway and Desert Inn Road. (702) 735-8268.* This enclosed mall has more than 1 million square feet of shopping space, making it the largest shopping center in Nevada. Major department stores include the Broadway Southwest, Dillards, JC Penney and Sears, as well as 123 other stores. Hours are 10 a.m. to 9 p.m. Monday through Friday, 10 a.m. to 6 p.m. Saturday, noon to 5 p.m. Sunday.

Fashion Show Mall, *Las Vegas Boulevard South and Spring Mountain Road. (702) 369-8382.* The enclosed, two-level mall houses 140 shops, restaurants and boutiques. Major department stores include Bullock's, Dillards, Neiman-Marcus, Robinsons-May and Saks Fifth Avenue. Extensive landscaping at the front of the mall helps create an expansive pedestrian promenade. A lighted underground parking facility holds more than 1500 cars. Mall hours are 10 a.m. to 9 p.m. Monday through Friday, 10 a.m. to 7 p.m. Saturday, and noon to 6 p.m. Sunday.

The Forum Shops at Caesars, *at Caesars Palace, 3570 Las Vegas Boulevard South. (702) 893-4800.* This upscale indoor mall features a Roman motif and more than 50 shops under a domed "sky" that changes colors. The shops include Ann Taylor, Vasari, Louis Vuitton, Gucci, Bernini, St. John, Cache and Bruno Magli, among others. There are also three art galleries and 11 restaurants. Hours are 10 a.m. to 11 p.m. daily, except January 1 and December 25 when the shops close at 6 p.m.

Las Vegas Factory Stores, *9155 Las Vegas Boulevard South. (702) 897-9090.* This shopping center features 28 factory outlet stores that include Florsheim, Geoffrey Beene, Corning/Revere, Sedona Indian Traders, Toy Liquidators and Izod, among others. Hours are 10 a.m. to 8 p.m. Monday through Saturday, and 10 a.m. to 6 p.m. Sunday.

Meadows Mall, *4300 Meadows Lane. (702) 878-3331; (702) 878-4849.* This enclosed mall contains Broadway Southwest, Dillards, JC Penney and Sears department stores, as well as 144 shops, restaurants and boutiques. In the mall center court is a 38-foot-diameter 1920s-style, hand-painted carousel. Rides cost 50¢ per person. Mall hours are 10 a.m. to 9 p.m. Monday through Friday, 10 a.m. to 6 p.m. Saturday, noon to 5 p.m. Sunday; extended hours during the December holiday season.

Robert Brown

The Forum Shops at Caesars Palace offers upscale shopping in a Roman village setting.

MARRIAGE INFORMATION

Love is always in the air in Las Vegas. It is in this desert community that a marriage license is issued every six minutes, and couples tie the knot with none other than Elvis (well, almost) presiding over the ceremonies. Seven days a week, 24 hours a day on weekends (correct change required), wedding vows are taken at drive-up windows, bungee jumping platforms, and from helicopters, boats, hotel suites, churches and dozens of wedding chapels. For better or worse, Las Vegas is the marriage capital of the world.

Marriages in Las Vegas total over 85,000 per year, due in part to the ease of obtaining a license. The bride and groom must simply appear at the Marriage Bureau office, located in the courthouse at 200 South 3rd Street, to purchase the license. No legal residency is required. Blood tests are not needed, and there is no waiting period. Persons aged 16 through 18 must have the consent of their parents or legal guardians. If the bride or groom was previously married, divorce must be final in the state in which it was granted; no papers are required. The office is open from 8 a.m. to midnight Monday through Thursday; continuously (24 hours) from 8 a.m. Friday to midnight Sunday; 24 hours on holidays. The license fee is $35; correct change required. For information, call the Marriage Bureau office at (702) 455-3156.

Marriage ceremonies can be performed by the Commissioner of Civil Marriages, 309 South 3rd Street, or in one of the many wedding chapels in town (35 at last count). The commissioner's office charges $35, and their hours are the same as the county clerk's office. Wedding chapel fees depend on the elaborateness of the ceremony. Some of the large hotel/casino complexes have wedding chapels on the grounds. For a list of wedding chapels see the Las Vegas telephone directory yellow pages under "Wedding."

Las Vegas wedding chapels perform both traditional and unique ceremonies. This couple chose a bicycle built for five.

ANNUAL EVENTS

In addition to entertainment at the major resort and casino facilities, Las Vegas offers a wide variety of other activities on its calendar. For information on any of the listed events, contact the Las Vegas News Bureau at (702) 735-3611.

The San Diego Padres' Pacific Coast League team, the Las Vegas Stars, plays its home games at Cashman Field from early April through mid-September. The University of Nevada, Las Vegas' NCAA "Runnin' Rebels" Big West basketball team begins its season at the Thomas and Mack Center in November and plays through February; the university's NCAA football team plays at the Sam Boyd Silver Bowl September through November. The Silver Bowl also hosts motocross competitions from June to Labor Day. AWA wrestling competitions are held at the Showboat Hotel, and throughout the year WBA and WBC boxing matches are held at the Las Vegas Hilton, Caesars Palace and MGM Grand hotels; ESPN Top Rank boxing matches are held at Bally's Casino Resort.

Casino tournaments in bridge, blackjack, slot play, craps, poker, gin rummy and bowling take place monthly rotating from one casino to another.

Anyone interested in these tournaments should contact the hotel or venue directly for dates and play information; room reservations should be made well in advance, as room space is often at a premium during a tournament.

February—
Sam's Town Annual Chili Cook-Off; Las Vegas International Marathon.

March—
Nissan Mint 400 Annual Desert Off-Road Race; Craft Festival at Cashman Field; Hoover Dam Square Dances; St. Patrick's Day Parade and Block Party; Angel Plane Air Show.

April—
The Auction (antique cars); Clark County Fair (Logandale); Industrial Days (Henderson); Las Vegas Senior Golf Tournament; Spring Jamboree (Boulder City).

May—
Elks Helldorado Days PRCA Rodeo and Western Festival; Clark County Artists' Show (Boulder City); Snow Mountain Powwow.

July—
Damboree (Boulder City).

August—
Festival in the Pines (Mt. Charleston).

September—
Jerry Lewis Telethon; San Gennaro Feast; Floyd Lamb State Park Western Fun Days;

World's Oldest Waterski Race (Lake Mead).

October—
Jaycees State Fair; Las Vegas Invitational PGA Tournament; Imperial Palace Antique Auto Run; North Las Vegas Fairshow and Nevada Championship Hot Air Balloon Races; Boy Scouts of America Scout-O-Rama; Las Vegas Indian Days; Art in the Park (Boulder City); Nevada Day Parade.

December—
Las Vegas Bowl; Lake Mead Boat Parade of Lights; Circus Circus Nevada Chili Cook-off; National Finals Rodeo; Christmas Parade (Boulder City).

Las Vegas News Bureau

National Finals Rodeo week brings PRCA events to Thomas & Mack Center.

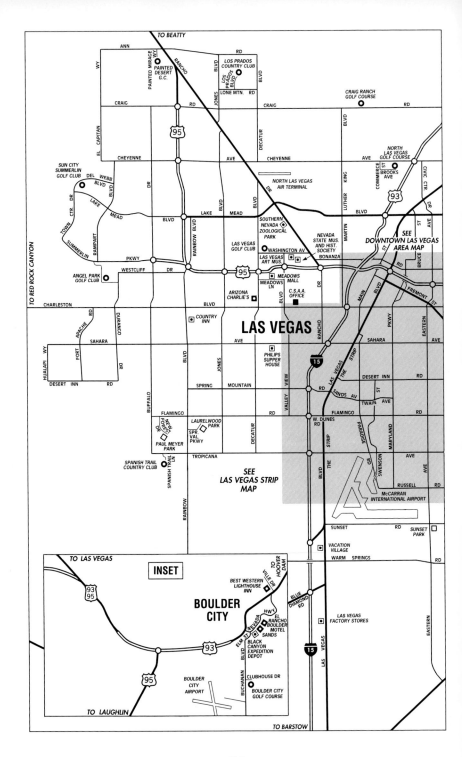

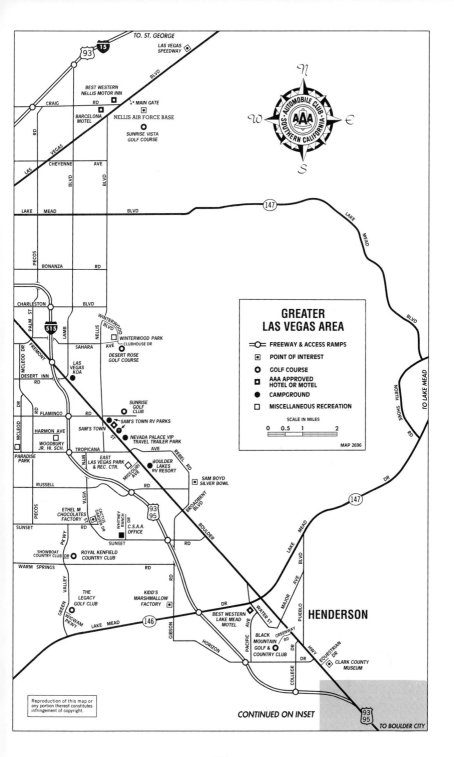

35

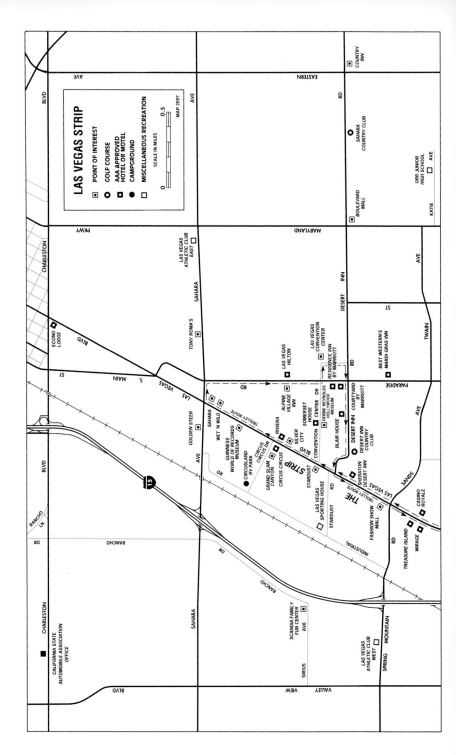

LAS VEGAS STRIP

POINT OF INTEREST ⊡
GOLF COURSE ⊙
AAA APPROVED HOTEL OR MOTEL ◻
CAMPGROUND ●
MISCELLANEOUS RECREATION ◻

SCALE IN MILES

0   0.5

MAP 2697

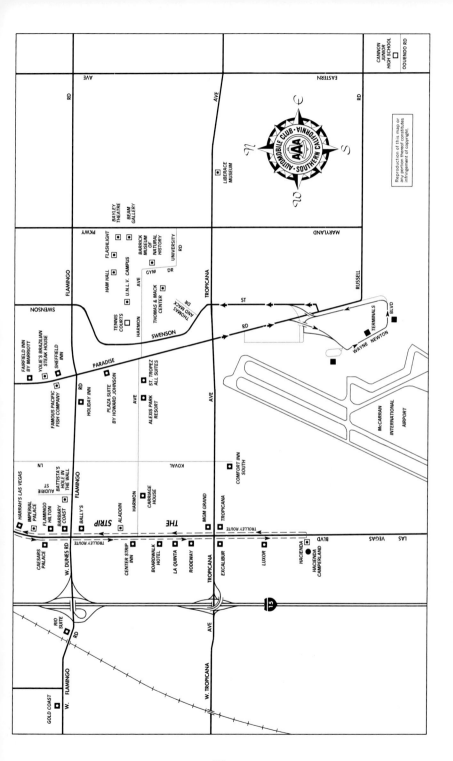

37

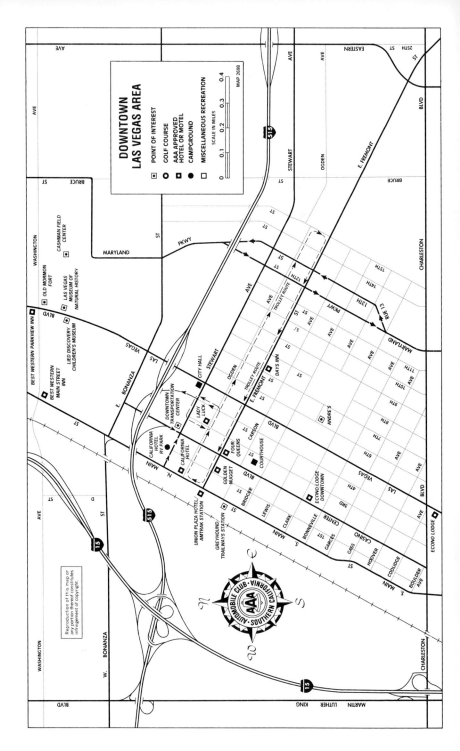

DOWNTOWN
LAS VEGAS AREA

POINT OF INTEREST
GOLF COURSE
AAA APPROVED
HOTEL OR MOTEL
CAMPGROUND
MISCELLANEOUS RECREATION

SCALE IN MILES
0   0.1   0.2   0.3   0.4

MAP 2698

38

POINTS OF INTEREST

There's a lot more to Las Vegas than the flashy casinos and big production shows, after all it is the "entertainment capital of the world." The city is also home to an increasing number of museums, amusement parks, sporting facilities, and even a small zoo.

LAS VEGAS

BUCCANEER BAY and MUTINY BAY, *Treasure Island, 3300 Las Vegas Boulevard South. (702) 894-7111.* Located at the entrance of Treasure Island is the spectacular Buccaneer Bay where visitors are treated to free, hourly sea battles between an 80-foot-long pirate ship and a British frigate. A separate attraction at the hotel is Mutiny Bay, an 18,000 square foot pirate-themed entertainment complex that features video games, pinball and electronic games.

CASHMAN FIELD CENTER, *just north of downtown at 850 Las Vegas Boulevard North. (702) 386-7100.* Its convention facilities include two exhibition halls with over 49,000 square feet of space each, plus a 1940-seat theater. The Las Vegas Stars, the San Diego Padres AAA Pacific Coast League team, play at this location from early April through Labor Day.

Old Las Vegas Mormon Fort State Park, *East Washington Avenue and Las Vegas Boulevard North. (702) 486-3511.* The fort, built by Mormons in 1855, is the oldest historic site in southern Nevada. It provided shelter for gold-seekers and other travelers along the Salt Lake-Los Angeles Trail. The fort was left to the Indians after the gold rush, and was restored and used as a railroad junction post for a railroad that pre-dated the Union Pacific. Its promise of railroad traffic helped launch a town site. Today a restored fort stands on the site along with the Cashman Field Center. Turn-of-the-century antiques are displayed, and guided tours are available. Call for hours. Donation $1 for adults, 50¢ for children.

DEBBIE REYNOLDS' HOLLY-WOOD MUSEUM, *Debbie Reynolds Hollywood Hotel/ Casino, 305 Convention Center Drive. (702) 734-0711.* Thousands of Hollywood props, rare film clips and movie costumes are displayed, including a test pair of ruby slippers from the Wizard of Oz, and costumes worn by actors John Wayne, Marilyn Monroe, Claudette Colbert and Elizabeth Taylor. As of press time, the museum was still under construction. Call the hotel for more information.

GRAND SLAM CANYON, *adjacent to the Circus Circus Hotel-Casino, 2880 Las Vegas Boulevard South, (702) 734-0410.* A five-acre climate-controlled indoor amusement park. The attractions include the nation's only double-loop, double-corkscrew indoor roller coaster, a soaking water ride, and a 45-foot-high tubular slide. More rides are planned for the near future, including a $6 million replica of the space shuttle. The amusement park is open daily from 10 a.m. to 10 p.m. Admission is based on a point system; $10 is enough for one turn on each ride. For those who just want to look, an admission price of $3 is also available, and that fee can be applied toward a meal at the on-site restaurant.

GUINNESS WORLD OF RECORDS MUSEUM AND GIFT SHOP, *2780 Las Vegas Boulevard South. (702) 792-3766.* Rare videos and artifacts commemorate the world's fastest, greatest, rarest and richest feats from the worlds of entertainment, art, sports and science. Literally thousands of records can be accessed from the "Guinness World of Records" and "World of Sports" data banks. Displays offer visitors the chance to match their height with the world's tallest man and shortest woman, and their weight

Imperial Palace

The Imperial Palace Auto Collection features a changing exhibit of more than 200 of their 800 classic, antique and special-interest autos, trucks and motorcycles.

with that of the world's heaviest man. The "world" of Las Vegas is featured in a display highlighting the city's history, its casinos and entertainers. The museum is open daily; call for hours. Admission is $4.95 for adults; $3.95 for senior citizens, students and military; $2.95 for children ages 5-11.

IMPERIAL PALACE AUTO COLLECTION, *Imperial Palace Hotel, 3535 Las Vegas Boulevard South. (702) 794-3174.* This auto museum, located on the fifth level of the hotel's parking facility, features more than 200 antique, classic and special-interest autos, antique trucks and motorcycles, and cars once owned by gangsters and world-famous celebrities. It also houses the world's largest collection of Model J Duesenbergs. The most valuable car is a 1939 Mercedes touring sedan once owned by Adolf Hitler and estimated to be worth more than $600,000. The collection contains more than 800 vehicles, which are rotated on a monthly basis. The museum is open daily from 9:30 a.m. to 11:30 p.m. Admission is $6.95 for adults; $3 for senior citizens and children ages 5-11. **Discount** (see page 2).

LAS VEGAS ART MUSEUM, *located in picturesque Lorenzi Park at 3333 West Washington Avenue. (702) 647-4300.* The work of local, national and international artists is featured individually and in group showings and competitions. In addition to the monthly changing exhibits, this small museum contains a permanent collection and a young people's gallery; it also sponsors art classes and programs. The museum is open Tuesday through Saturday from 10 a.m. to 3 p.m.,

and Sunday from noon to 3 p.m. (summer hours may vary); closed Monday and holidays.

LAS VEGAS CONVENTION CENTER, *3150 Paradise Road. (702) 892-0711.* With 1.3 million square feet of meeting and exhibit space, the convention center is one of the largest single-level facilities in the country. A rotunda, four large meeting halls, numerous meeting rooms of various sizes and an on-site restaurant make it possible for the center to host groups of less than 100 people or conventions of more than 100,000 people.

LAS VEGAS MUSEUM OF NATURAL HISTORY, *900 Las Vegas Boulevard North. (702) 384-3466.* The museum features life-sized skeletal and animated dinosaurs, modern-day animals from North America and Africa, and a wildlife art collection that includes paintings, bronzes, marble sculpture and wood carvings of wildfowl. The museum is open daily from 9 a.m. to 4 p.m. Admission is $5 for adults; $4 for senior citizens, military and students; $2.50 for ages 4-12; children under 4 are admitted free.

LAS VEGAS SPEEDWAY, *6000 Las Vegas Boulevard North. (702) 643-3333.* The speedway can accommodate drag racing, as well as oval and course racing events. The National Hot Rod Association (NHRA) Winston Championship Drag Racing Gambler Nationals are held in October, and other events are scheduled throughout the year. Call for program information and ticket prices.

LIBERACE MUSEUM, *2 miles east of the Strip at 1775 East Tropicana Boulevard. (702) 798-5595.* The museum collection of memorabilia, antiques and classic cars includes Liberace's million-dollar wardrobe and extensive fur collection, his gold and diamond stage jewelry (including a diamond and platinum candelabra ring) and a Baldwin grand piano inlaid with thousands of etched mirror tiles showcased on a revolving stage for live concerts. Of particular interest are a Czar Nicolas uniform with 22-karat gold braiding, a piano that Chopin once played and a crucifix presented to Liberace by Pope Pius XII. The museum also includes a re-creation of Liberace's office and bedroom, and a library displaying his miniature piano collection and a photographic history of his life. The museum is open Monday through Saturday from 10 a.m. to 5 p.m., Sunday from 1 to 5 p.m. Admission is $6.50 for adults; $4.50 for senior citizens; $3.50 for students; and $2 for ages 6-12. All children must be accompanied by an adult. Proceeds from the museum go to the non-profit Liberace Foundation for the Performing and Creative Arts. **Discount** (see page 2).

LIED DISCOVERY CHILDREN'S MUSEUM, *833 Las Vegas Boulevard North. (702) 382-3445.* The museum features over 100 hands-on exhibits that allow children to explore the world they live in. Play areas include "Places and Spaces," "What Can I Be?" and

Liberace Museum

Many of Liberace's sequined, rhinestoned and feathered costumes and much of his stage jewelry are on display at the Liberace Museum.

The pyramid-shaped Luxor Hotel-Casino features three levels of family-oriented attractions.

"Everyday Living," as well as the Toddler Tower, the Bubble Pavilion and a story phone. The museum is open 10 a.m. to 5 p.m. Tuesday, Thursday, Friday and Saturday; 10 a.m. to 7 p.m. Wednesday; and noon to 5 p.m. Sunday. Admission is $5 for adults; $4 for senior citizens, children ages 12-17 and military; $3 for ages 3-11. Children 2 and under are admitted free.

LUXOR ENTERTAINMENT COMPLEX, *at the Luxor Hotel-Casino, 3900 Las Vegas Boulevard South. (702) 262-4555.* Three levels of Egyptian-themed attractions that include a series of participatory films that use motion simulators and large-screen film projections, a video arcade, replicas of early Egyptian artifacts, and a full-size reproduction of King Tut's tomb. The shows screen daily every 30 minutes beginning at 10 a.m. Admission is $5 per person.

MGM GRAND ADVENTURES, *at the MGM Grand Hotel Casino and Theme Park, 3799 Las Vegas Boulevard South. (702) 891-7777.* A 33-acre theme park that features thrilling roller coaster and water rides, bumper cars and a journey through a haunted mine. There are also celebrity lookalikes, strolling performers, musical acts, nine themed streets, restaurants and shops. The theme park is open daily 10 a.m. to 6 p.m., and later during the summer months. Call for admission price information.

Scandia Family Fun Center features three 18-hole miniature golf courses, Indy-style racers, bumper boats and a large video-game arcade.

NELLIS AIR FORCE BASE, *main gate at Las Vegas Boulevard and Craig Road. (702) 652-1110.* Nellis, a weapons testing and tactical fighter training center, is also the home of the "Thunderbirds," the Air Force's precision flying team. Although based here, the Thunderbirds are often away performing at air shows throughout the country, but they do perform at the Nellis AFB open house held every two years.

Thunderbird Museum, *located on the base (directions are given at the main gate). (702) 652-4018.* A public tour of the museum is offered Tuesday and Thursday at 2 p.m. The tour includes a short program, a videotape movie, and a tour of the museum which includes photographs and a static display of an F-16. The museum is closed the last two weeks of December.

NEVADA STATE MUSEUM AND HISTORICAL SOCIETY, *in Lorenzi Park at 700 Twin Lakes Drive. (702) 486-5205.* Three main galleries focus on the history, anthropology and biology of the southern Nevada area. Two galleries house changing exhibits on a variety of topics. A research library and museum store are also located here. The museum is open daily from 8:30 a.m. to 4:30 p.m. Admission is $2 for adults; free for those under 18.

OMNIMAX® THEATRE, *at Caesars Palace, 3570 Las Vegas Boulevard South. (702) 731-7900.* The theater, with 368 seats, contains a movie screen that covers 86 percent of the interior space. Seats recline to a 27-degree angle, allowing the audience an unparalleled view of the screen. A six-track stereophonic sound system with 16 speaker banks and 86 individual speakers provides sound throughout the theater. There are hourly showings of features Sunday through Thursday from 2 to 10 p.m., Friday and Saturday from 1 to 11 p.m.; programs change regularly. Admission is $5.50 for adults and $3.50 for senior citizens, military, students and children 12 and under.

SCANDIA FAMILY FUN CENTER, *on the west side of I-15 south of Sahara Avenue, at 2900 Sirius Avenue. (702) 364-0070.* This amusement center features miniature Indy-type race cars, three elaborate 18-hole miniature golf courses, bumper boats, baseball batting cages and a large video-game arcade. During the summer the center is open 10 a.m. to midnight Sunday through Thursday, and 10 a.m. to 1:30 a.m. Friday and Saturday. In winter the hours are 10 a.m. to 10:30 p.m. Sunday through Thursday, 10 a.m. to midnight Friday and Saturday.

SOUTHERN NEVADA ZOOLOGICAL PARK, *1775 North Rancho Drive, corner of Melody Lane, about three miles northwest of downtown. (702) 648-5955; 647-4685.* A small zoological-botanical park, especially appealing to children. The zoo displays a collection of mostly small animals and birds, including Barbary apes, African green grivit monkeys, an African lion, Bengal tiger, cougar, coyote, alligator, and a collection of exotic birds and talking parrots. There is also a children's petting zoo featuring Pygmy goats. A snack bar and gift shop are located on the grounds. The park is open daily 9 a.m. to 5 p.m. Admission is $5 for adults; $3 for ages 2-12 and over 60.

STRATOSPHERE TOWER, *Vegas World Hotel-Casino, 2000 Las Vegas Boulevard South. (702) 382-2000.* The Stratosphere Tower, currently under construction, is slated for completion in December 1994. Rising 1,012 feet above the Strip, it will be the tallest observation tower in the United States — and 29 feet taller than the Eiffel Tower in Paris. In addition to its outside observation platform (which will feature a see-through floor), its tower-top "pod" will include a 400-seat restaurant, a cocktail lounge, four wedding chapels and a whirling thrill ride. Hours and prices have not yet been established.

UNIVERSITY OF NEVADA, LAS VEGAS, *4505 Maryland Parkway. (702) 895-3011.* More than 19,000 students attend classes on the 335-acre campus. The school's curriculum covers courses in fine arts, performing arts, mathematics, engineering, English, science, health and social sciences, business, hotel administration and the humanities. The university's first building, Maude Frazier Hall, opened its doors in 1957. After a brief stint as Nevada Southern University, the campus was given autonomy and equality with the University of Nevada, Reno in 1968 and renamed in 1969. Campus tours are given by the admissions office; for information visit Maude Frazier Hall, Room 114, or call (702) 895-3443.

A brochure for a self-guided arboretum tour of the campus is available from the UNLV news and publications office, the Museum of Natural History and the grounds department.

Artemus W. Ham Concert Hall and **Judy Bayley Theatre,** *at the north end of Academic Mall.* These two facilities form the campus' Center for the Performing Arts. The Masters Series programs at the concert hall often feature nationally known touring companies in symphonic music, ballet and opera. The hall also serves as home to the Las Vegas Symphonic and Chamber Music Society, whose season from September through April includes symphony, chamber and pop music concerts, as well as opera. Tickets range from $8 to $125. The Judy Bayley Theatre is home to the Nevada Dance Theatre. Their four-program schedule runs from October through May. Tickets range from $12 to $25. For schedule and ticket information call (702) 895-3801.

Donna Beam Fine Art Gallery, *in Alta Ham Fine Arts Building, Room 130.* The gallery hosts changing exhibitions by students, faculty and invited artists. Hours are 8 a.m. to 5 p.m. Monday through Friday; closed major holidays. Admission is free.

Flashlight, a 38-foot-high steel sculpture fashioned by Claes Oldenberg and Coosje van Bruggen, is located in the plaza at the north end of Academic Mall near Artemus W. Ham Concert Hall.

Marjorie Barrick Museum of Natural History, *on campus; turn east on Harmon Avenue off Swenson Street.* The museum encompasses permanent exhibits on the archaeology, geology and biology of the desert Southwest, an outdoor botanical garden and displays of indigenous live animals. The museum is open 9 a.m. to 5 p.m. Monday through Friday, 10 a.m. to 5 p.m. Saturday. Admission is free. (702) 895-3381.

Sam Boyd Silver Bowl, *off campus, off US 93/95 (use Russell Road exit), in Silver Bowl Regional Park.* The stadium is home for the university's NCAA football team from September through November. It also hosts motocross competitions and concerts in the summer. For ticket information call (702) 895-3900.

Thomas and Mack Center, *off Tropicana Avenue at Swenson Street.* This 18,500-seat indoor arena hosts sporting events, concerts and shows. From December through February it provides the home court for the school's NCAA "Runnin' Rebels" Big West basketball team. For events schedule and ticket information call (702) 895-3900.

WET 'N WILD, *2601 Las Vegas Boulevard South. (702) 734-0088.* This 26-acre, family-oriented water playground features "Willy Willy," a hydra-hurricane ride, "Banzai Banzai," a water roller coaster, and "Bomb Bay," a 76-foot-high water slide. In addition, there are rapids, a 500,000-gallon wave pool, a surf lagoon and a children's pool. Areas for sunbathing and picnicking are also available. The hours are 10 a.m. to 6 p.m. April through September; extended hours in June, July and August. All-day adult admission is $18.95; $14.95 for ages 3-9; free for children under 3. **Discount** (see page 2).

SURROUNDING AREAS

Beyond the Strip and downtown areas are other, less familiar aspects of Las Vegas. No more than 90 minutes' drive from the heart of town are the desert wonders of Valley of Fire State Park and the mountain greenery of Toiyabe National Forest. Hoover Dam, an extremely popular tourist attraction, is only 30 miles from Las Vegas, and stretching behind this man-made colossus is 110-mile-long Lake Mead, a center for water sports. Near the north end of the lake visitors can view petroglyphs left by American Indians hundreds of years ago.

CLARK COUNTY MUSEUM, *13 miles southeast of Las Vegas at 1830 South Boulder Highway (US 93/95) in Henderson. (702) 455-7955.* This county historical museum encompasses the new Southwest-style exhibit center, Heritage Street, a collection of historic homes and commercial buildings, and an outdoor ghost town. The museum is open daily from 9 a.m. to 4:30 p.m.; closed January 1 and December 25. Admission is $1 for adults; 50¢ for

seniors and ages 6-15; children under 6 are admitted free.

ETHEL M CHOCOLATES FACTORY, *6 miles southeast of the Strip at 2 Cactus Garden Drive, off Sunset Way, in Henderson. (702) 458-8864.* Free self-guided tours of the factory offer a behind-the-scenes look at the ingredients and machinery used in the candy-making process. Adjacent to the factory is a cactus display and botanical garden. The factory and garden are open daily from 8:30 a.m. to 7 p.m.; closed Thanksgiving and December 25.

FLOYD LAMB STATE PARK, *15 miles north of Las Vegas off US 95. (702) 486-5413.* Floyd Lamb State Park encompasses 2040 acres including the Tule Springs Ranch, four small lakes and the surrounding natural desert area. The park is open daily from 8 a.m. to dusk; a day-use fee is charged. A self-guided tour of Tule Springs Ranch includes the caretaker's house, the stables and dairy barn, the adobe hut built by John Herbert Nay, the guest house, swimming pool, gazebo, pump

The Automobile Club of Southern California prints several publications that may be useful when visiting areas surrounding Las Vegas. For map coverage of these areas refer to the Auto Club's *San Bernardino County and Las Vegas Area* map or the *Guide to Colorado River.* Public and privately operated campgrounds are listed in the camping section of this book, and some of the areas are also covered on the *Guide to Colorado River.* These publications are free to Auto Club members at all Auto Club district offices in California and Nevada.

house, root cellar, spring house and alfalfa barn, among other buildings. Self-guided hiking trails traverse tree-shaded groves and pass by the lakes. Fishing is permitted in all four lakes. Tule Lake is stocked with rainbow trout in winter and catfish in summer. Largemouth bass are native to all the lakes, but the catch is low. Swimming and boating are not allowed. Picnic tables and grills are located throughout the park and are available on a first come, first served basis.

The Tule Springs area has long been known as one of the best Pleistocene fossil sites in western North America. Remains found here have included giant sloths, bison, camels, horses and mammoths. Man's first presence in the area, however, only dates back 10,000 to 11,000 years. Today that presence is much more in evidence. The area that is now Floyd Lamb State Park was used as a watering stop by American Indians and local prospectors, and as a rest stop for horses on the Bullfrog Stage Line to Rhyolite. John Herbert Nay began farming the land in 1916, but sold the land in 1928. It remained vacant until 1941 when Jacob Goumond turned it into a working ranch.

When Nevada's divorce laws became the most liberal in the country by requiring only a six-week residency, Goumond saw a chance to make money with a "dude" ranch. Divorcees who came to live out their residency requirements occupied themselves with horseback riding, swimming, tennis, hayrides, barbecues, dances and a shooting range. But even as a dude ranch, Tule Springs remained a working ranch. Livestock included a herd of cattle, dairy cows, horses, chickens, turkeys and pigs. Fruits and vegetables were grown year round and 100 acres was cultivated in alfalfa. Ranch denizens today include peacocks, ducks, geese, chickens and a herd of cattle.

HOOVER DAM, *30 miles southeast of Las Vegas via US 93/95 on US 93. (702) 293-8367.* Completed in 1935, the 726-foot-high dam is considered one of the engineering wonders of the world. Not only did the dam help control the sometimes violent Colorado River, it provided a cheap source of electricity which aided the development of Las Vegas and Southern California. Thirty-five-minute guided tours of the dam and its hydroelectric turbines are conducted daily from 8 a.m. to 6:45 p.m. Memorial Day through Labor Day, and from 9 a.m. to 4:15 p.m. during the rest of the year. Admission is $3 for adults, $1.50 for seniors, and children under 12 are admitted free.

KIDD'S MARSHMALLOW FACTORY, *8203 Gibson Road, in Henderson. (702) 564-5400.* This self-guided tour offers visitors a chance to view the entire marshmallow-making process from start to finish. A free bag of marshmallows is given to each visitor at the end of the tour. The factory is open daily from 9:30 a.m. to 4:30 p.m., and the tour is free.

LAKE MEAD NATIONAL RECREATION AREA, *approximately 20 miles east of Las Vegas.* The six major recreation areas on the lake are **Boulder Beach,** 28 miles southeast via US 93 and SR 166; **Las Vegas Bay,** 17 miles east via SR 147 (Lake Mead Boulevard); **Callville Bay,** 29 miles east via SR 147, North Shore Road and Callville Bay Road; **Echo Bay,** 54 miles northeast via SR 147, North Shore Road and unnamed

The 726-foot-high Hoover Dam is located 30 miles southeast of Las Vegas.

road to Echo Bay; **Overton Beach,** 60 miles northeast via I-15 and SR 169; and **Temple Bar,** Arizona, 75 miles southeast via US 93 and Temple Bar Road. For information on Lake Mohave see *Points of Interest* under Laughlin.

Alan Bible Visitor Center, *4 miles northeast of Boulder City on US 93. (702) 293-8906.* The entire Lake Mead National Recreation Area is administered by the National Park Service. The center is the single best source of information on the recreation area and contains a botanical garden and exhibits on natural history. A number of publications about the area can be purchased here. The center is open daily from 8:30 a.m. to 4:30 p.m.; closed January 1, Thanksgiving and December 25. Admission is free.

Caution: Care should be taken when traveling in this area.

- Desert thunderstorms in summer and fall can produce both lightning and flash floods. Never camp in a wash or low-lying area. Never drive across flooded roads; many roads have been posted flash-flood areas.

- Summer heat can cause heat exhaustion and heat stroke in a person and cripple a car that does not have adequate coolant in the cooling system. Refer to Desert Driving Hints under *Transportation.*

- Rattlesnakes, scorpions and Gila monsters (a type of lizard) are indigenous to this area, and all are poisonous. They usually will not attack you unless cornered, but caution should be taken to avoid them.

49

- Drive only on paved roads or on unpaved roads marked with yellow arrows. Check with rangers about road conditions before traveling unpaved roads.

For emergency assistance, contact a ranger or call the 24-hour emergency phone number (702) 293-8932.

One of the largest man-made lakes in the world, Lake Mead is 110 miles long and has a shoreline five times that length. Much of the surrounding landscape is rugged desert interspersed with often stark grayish-purple mountains, colorful red-rock canyons and a variety of desert shrubbery including cacti and creosote bushes. A scenic drive along the north shore of the lake (North Shore Road) and a small section of the south shore (Lake Shore Highway) provides panoramic views. (Many of the picturesque coves and bays, however, are accessible only by boat.) Mild weather throughout most of the year is punctuated by hot dry summers when temperatures often reach over 100 degrees. Recreational activities encompass fishing, swimming, waterskiing, camping, hiking, picnicking, scuba diving, sailing, powerboating and houseboating.

North Shore Road, running north from Lake Mead Boulevard (SR 147) to Echo Bay and Overton Beach, offers a **scenic drive** and often a spectacular view of the surrounding mountains and hills. Browns, burnt reds and black rocks are contrasted with the stark off-whites and tans of this intriguing landscape. Each hill is seemingly formed from a different material, but all are the product of an active geologic past. Many of the hills are covered with square chunks of black volcanic rock that appear to have rained down from a nearby extinct caldera. Where the hillsides have been cut away for access roads to the lake, such as the road to Callville Bay, the sediments appear to have been "juiced." The red and black rocks that dominate the landscape speak of the high iron and magnesium content of the volcanic debris. The local sedimentary rocks, such as the sandstone layers evidenced in the nearby hills, were laid down by water and then uplifted at a later time. A high iron content is also evidenced there, often by an entire range of stark red hills. The vividness of the colors of the rocks seen on this drive can often vary not only with the time of day, but also with the direction of travel. What may appear dull and drab through the front windshield may look entirely different in the rear view mirror. Drive carefully— the greatest hazard here is looking at the landscape instead of where one is driving.

Boat cruises on Lake Mead offering a view of Sentinel Island and Hoover Dam are available on the *Desert Princess* sternwheeler. The 90-minute tours leave daily from Lake Mead Marina at 11:30 a.m., 1:30 and 3:30 p.m. (seasonal). The fare is $12 for adults; children under 12, $5. Evening dinner/dance cruises are $32.50 per person; cocktail cruises (seasonal) are $23 for adults and $10.50 for children; breakfast cruises are $16.50 for adults and $8 for children. Reservations are recommended for all cruises. For more information contact Lake Mead Cruises at (702) 293-6180.

Lake Mohave **raft trips** from the bottom of Hoover Dam south to Willow Beach, Arizona, are available February through November and leave from the Expedition Depot at 1297 Nevada Highway in Boulder City. The three-hour trip through Black Canyon to Willow Beach is fully narrated and traverses Ringbolt Rapids (complete round-trip takes 5½ hours). Lunch is provided at Willow Beach, and then passengers are returned to the Expedition Depot by bus. Raft trips are $64.95 per person (includes lunch); children under 12, $35 (includes lunch). Reservations are advised. For hotel pickup in Las Vegas see the Gray Line Tours listing under *Guided Tours*. For more information contact Black Canyon, Inc. at (800) 845-3833 or (702) 293-3776.

Houseboats can be rented at the Callville Bay Resort, (800) 255-5561, or at Echo Bay Resort, (800) 752-9669. For details contact the resorts directly. A deposit is required, and reservations should be made several months in advance.

Lake Mead Fish Hatchery, *9½ miles north of Boulder City on SR 166 (Lakeshore Highway). (702) 486-6738.* The visitor center is open daily from 8 a.m. to 4 p.m. Displays at the center explain production methods. **Sportfish** in the lake include striped bass, catfish, crappie and bluegill. The lake offers an open season on all fish year round, and rangers can help point out the best fishing areas. To fish from shore, a state fishing license is required; fishing from a boat requires a state license from one state (Arizona or Nevada) and a special stamp from the other. Most marinas sell licenses and stamps, as well as bait and tackle.

LOST CITY MUSEUM, *in Overton, 60 miles northeast of Las Vegas via I-15 and SR 169. (702) 397-2193.* This museum offers visitors a chance to see both original American Indian relics and faithful reconstructions of Pueblo dwellings. The last 10,000 years have seen several cultures in residence, including hunters and gatherers represented by the Gypsum Cave People, Ancient Basketmakers, Early Pueblos and most recently the Paiute Indians, who came to the area about 900 years ago. Hundreds of ruins near the museum have not yet been excavated, and as the delicate process of unearthing the remains continues, more and more is revealed about the past inhabitants of the area. The museum is open daily from 8:30 a.m. to 4:30 p.m. (closed major holidays). Admission is $2 for adults, free for ages 18 and under.

RED ROCK CANYON NATIONAL CONSERVATION AREA, *15 miles west of Las Vegas via SR 159 (West Charleston Boulevard) or 20 miles west of Las Vegas via SR 160 (Blue Diamond Road).* This scenic area, administered by the Bureau of Land Management, includes a 13-mile, one-way scenic drive off of SR 159, a visitor center, hiking trails, panoramic overlooks, wildlife and American Indian rock art.

Visitor Center, *located at the beginning of the scenic drive. (702) 363-1921.* Hours are 8:30 a.m. to 4:30 p.m. daily. The center, operated by the Bureau of Land Management, offers displays and materials on natural, cultural and geologic topics, scheduled activities and information about recreation in the surrounding areas.

Traveling Tips:

- Thunderstorms, especially in summer and early fall, can produce both lightning and flash floods. Never drive across flooded roads or camp in low-lying areas.

- Climbing on sandstone requires equipment and experience. Soft sandstone often crumbles and can be dangerous to climbers.

- Heat, cold and dehydration can take their toll on hikers. Carry one gallon of water for each person for each day. Summer days can bring extreme heat, and temperatures drop rapidly at night.

- All natural and historic features are protected by federal law. This includes animals, plants, rocks and American Indian artifacts. Do not damage, disturb or remove them.

A brochure is available at the visitor center for those wishing to bicycle in the park. Cyclists will find the Scenic Loop Drive a challenge for experienced riders. The steep undulating grades over the first five miles gain in altitude 1000 feet, followed by switchbacks at the top of the grade and then the 1000-foot drop in elevation over eight miles back to the visitor center. Round-trip mileage to the visitor center is 14$\frac{7}{10}$ miles. The one-way paved road assures riders of no oncoming traffic and since the road is two lanes wide, there is plenty of room for cars to pass cyclists. Weekend and holiday traffic, however, can be heavy. Beware of falling rocks in the switchbacks and loose pebbles and debris where the road crosses a wash. There is no repair facility or air for tires available in the park or in Blue Diamond, so come prepared to make your own repairs. A longer 37-mile ride is

Chris Hart

Scenic Loop Drive offers views of the vivid red sandstone in the Calico Hills.

also detailed in the brochure.

Scenic Loop Drive, *off SR 159,* is a one-way route that leaves near the visitor center, then returns to SR 159 about two miles south after traversing a 13-mile loop. The road is open daily from 8 a.m. to dusk. The drive offers a close look at the area's Aztec sandstone, plant life and the Keystone Thrust Fault. The fault occurred some 65 million years ago and is evidenced by the sharp contrast between the gray limestone and the red sandstone.

The first two pullouts on the scenic loop have short trails to the base of the Calico Hills, where seasonal rain pools can be found. These pools become temporary homes to small insects, insect larvae and fairy shrimp. Continuing along the drive, a trip to the Sandstone Quarry requires traveling along a short, graded dirt road. From this historic quarry, many small canyons can be explored. A short side road leads to the Willow Spring Picnic Area. A short hike from the road takes visitors to Lost Creek Canyon, where a year-round spring flows and occasionally provides a seasonal waterfall.

Farther along the drive is the Ice Box Canyon overlook. From the overlook, visitors may hike to a box canyon with steep walls which keep this canyon cooler than others in the area—hence the name. Seasonal pools and an occasional seasonal waterfall can also be found in the canyon.

From the Pine Creek Canyon overlook, last along the drive, a hiking trail leads to the remains of an old homestead. Also within the canyon are a creek and a large stand of ponderosa pine (at a record-low elevation).

Picnicking sites are located at Red Spring and Willow Spring. Charcoal fires are allowed at designated sites where grills are provided. Ground fires are prohibited. Primitive camping is permitted only at designated sites.

Spring Mountain Ranch State Park, *south of Scenic Loop Drive off SR 159. (702) 875-4141.* Now maintained by the Nevada Division of State Parks, the park at one time was a cattle ranch. Cattle still graze in the lush green pastures. The park is open for picnicking daily from 8 a.m. to dusk. The ranch house/visitor center is open 10 a.m. to 4 p.m. Friday through Monday and on holidays. The park sponsors evening theatrical events during the summer. Day-use fee.

TOIYABE NATIONAL FOREST, *35 miles northwest of Las Vegas via US 95 at the end of SR 156 and 157. (702) 873-8800.* Barely a 45-minute drive from the neon city of the desert, Toiyabe National Forest is a lush reprieve from high temperatures and stark landscapes. By taking the Spring Mountain Scenic Loop, visitors are exposed to a number of appealing sights as the road climbs to its maximum elevation of 8500 feet. At this elevation, the temperature in the forest is usually 30 degrees cooler than in Las Vegas. Weekend crowds attest to the forest's popularity with visitors; weekdays are usually quieter.

Caution: Portions of the national forest may close for the winter as early as October, depending on weather conditions, and tire chains may be required at any time during winter months.

Cathedral Rock, Old Mill and **Deer Creek** are enjoyable picnic areas if you pack a lunch. Comfortable walking shoes are also recommended since there are a number of hiking trails which lead through interesting areas of flora and fauna. Another feature is Mummy Mountain, so named because it looks like a huge mummy lying on its back.

Charleston Peak is one of the highest peaks in Nevada. A trail to the 11,918-foot summit of Charleston is usually open between June and October, though weather conditions can lengthen or shorten the hiking season considerably. You should be in good condition before attempting the climb since the gain in elevation from start to finish is almost 4000 feet, and the total round trip is over 18 miles.

Lee Canyon Ski Area, *located in the national forest 47 miles northwest of Las Vegas via US 95 and SR 156.*

(702) 646-0793. Facilities at this ski resort are open from 9:30 a.m. to 4 p.m. daily, Thanksgiving to Easter, and include rentals (alpine skis, boots and poles, snowboards), snowmaking, night skiing, GLM ski school, snack bar and day lodge. Runs are 15 percent novice, 65 percent intermediate and 20 percent advanced, with the longest run being ⁹⁄₁₀ mile. The vertical drop is 1000 feet. Three double chairs service the area; adult lift tickets are $25 for all day. The nearest AAA-approved accommodations are in Las Vegas. Remember that chains may be required when driving to this area.

VALLEY OF FIRE STATE PARK, *50 miles northeast of Las Vegas via I-15 and SR 169. (702) 397-2088.* **Visitor Center,** *located just off SR 169 midway into the park.* The center is open from 8:30 a.m. to 4:30 p.m. daily; closed January 1 and December

Las Vegas News Bureau

Visitors enjoy snow sports at Mt. Charleston during the winter months and escape to the higher elevations in summer when desert valley temperatures exceed 100 degrees.

Chris Hart

Valley of Fire State Park provides a striking display of red sandstone among the tan and gray earth tones of the desert.

25. Information is available about the park and its hiking trails. There are also displays on local fauna and an outdoor botanical garden.

Caution: Care should be taken when traveling in this area.

- Thunderstorms, especially in summer and early fall, can produce both lightning and flash floods. Never drive across flooded roads or camp in low-lying areas.

- All natural and historic features are protected. This includes animals, plants, rocks and American Indian artifacts. Do not damage, disturb or remove them.

- When hiking in canyon areas, care should be taken. Taking short-cuts may endanger your life. Never hike alone. Register at the visitor center before hiking back-country areas.

So named because of the effect of bright sunlight reflecting off red sandstone, Valley of Fire State Park contains dozens of unique geological formations, as well as the remnants of an ancient American Indian civilization.

The best examples of petroglyphs—pictures carved into rock—can be seen in the area of Atlatl Rock, located near the center of the park. Also well known for petroglyphs is Mouse's Tank, a canyon area named after an early renegade.

For fascinating natural formations, both Elephant Rock and Beehive Rocks offer distinct sights. There are also the remains of petrified logs in the park; thoughtless visitors, however, have taken so many samples that the amount of petrified wood is considerably depleted.

Because of its rare beauty, Valley of Fire has been used many times as the background for motion pictures. There are camping and picnicking facilities, plus hiking trails and a visitor center.

GUIDED TOURS

Taking a tour is an easy way to get a first-hand look at the many Las Vegas area attractions; since all of the arrangements, including transportation, are taken care of by the tour company.

The agencies listed below can help you explore the desert, experience the magnitude of Hoover Dam, cruise Lake Mead or view the spectacular Grand Canyon from the air. Tours generally last less than a day, though some of the trips to more distant places involve an overnight stay. In the latter case, accommodations are usually included in the quoted price. Be sure to contact the companies in advance for complete information and reservations since some excursions have seasonal limitations; most companies reserve the right to cancel any scheduled tour if there is an insufficient number of passengers.

Tours lasting from two to four hours are listed as "half day" tours; those five hours or longer are listed as "all day."

Tours listed are for visitors' information and convenience. The Automobile Club of Southern California does not recommend one tour company over another and cannot guarantee the services offered.

Grand Canyon Flights

In 1987 the U.S. Congress passed a law prohibiting flights below the canyon rim and directed the National Park Service (NPS) and the Federal Aviation Administration (FAA) to designate safe routes for flights over the national park area. NPS then proposed to the FAA that flight-free zones be established over 40 percent of the Grand Canyon, that air-tour operators be restricted to flying in specific corridors over the least-used parts of the park and that pilots be required to stay above the canyon rim. The law took effect in September 1988. A study is being conducted to assess the impact of these restrictions. According to a government spokesman, those flying over the canyon can still view much of the grandeur of the park. The main concerns are passenger safety and the level of noise the flights generate in the park.

Adventure Airlines,
P.O. Box 93445, Las Vegas, 89193-3445. (702) 736-7511; (800) 543-3077; FAX: (702) 736-2374. Hotel pickup. Children's rate available.

Grand Canyon (west end only)/ Air Tour (half day); Grand Canyon (west end only)/Air & Ground Tour with Indian barbecue (all day); Deluxe Valley of Fire/Hoover Dam, Arizona (land and air) tour, plus Lake Mead luncheon cruise and drive past Las Vegas celebrity homes (all day).

Air Nevada,
McCarran International Airport, P.O. Box 11105, Las Vegas, 89111.

(702) 736-8900; (800) 634-6377 outside NV. Hotel pickup. Children's rate available. **Discount** (see page 2). **(See ad above).**

Grand Canyon Deluxe Air & Ground Tour (all day); Grand Canyon Air Tour (half day); Grand Canyon "On Your Own" Air & Ground Tour (all day); Grand Canyon Overnight Tour (one or two days); Grand Canyon West Rim Air Tour (half day); Bryce Canyon Deluxe Air & Ground Tour (all day); Bryce Canyon/ Grand Canyon Deluxe Air & Ground Tour (all day); Bryce Canyon Overnight Tour.

Las Vegas News Bureau

Majestic Hoover Dam is a popular guided tour destination.

Eagle Canyon Airlines,
P.O. Box 96503, Las Vegas, 89193.
(702) 736-3333; (800) 446-4584.
Hotel pickup. Children's rate available. **Discount** (see page 2).
(See ad below.)

Grand Canyon Classic Air
Tour (half day); Grand Canyon
Premium Deluxe Air and
Ground Tour (all day); Grand
Canyon/Dinosaur Caverns Air
and Ground Tour (all day).

Gray Line Tours,
1550 S. Industrial Road, Las Vegas,
89102-2699. (702) 384-1234; FAX:
(702) 387-6401. Hotel pickup. All
tours are motorcoach tours.

Grand Canyon South Rim Overnight—March through October;
Grand Canyon Land and Air
Tour (all day); Grand Canyon
Air Tour/Colorado River (Black
Canyon) Raft Tour (all day);
Hoover Dam Tour (half day);
Hoover Dam/Lake Mead Cruise
(all day); Deluxe Hoover Dam/
Chocolate Factory (all day);
Lake Mead Champagne/Cocktail
Cruise (evenings) February
through November; Valley of
Fire/Lost City Museum Tour (all
day); Red Rock Canyon Tour (all
day); City Sightseeing Tour (all
day); Mini City Tour (half day);
Colorado River (Black Canyon)
Raft Tour (all day)—March
through mid-November
(weather permitting); Laughlin
Tour (all day); Laughlin "River
Gambler" Overnight Tour (one,
two or three nights).

Helicop-Tours,
135 East Reno Avenue, Suite F4,
Las Vegas, 89119. (702) 736-0606.
Hotel pickup. All tours are helicopter tours.

Grand Canyon/Hoover Dam/
Lake Mead Air Tour (half day);
Grand Canyon/Hoover Dam/
Lake Mead Champagne Picnic
Air Tour (half day); Grand
Canyon (west end only)/
Columbine Falls Air Tour (half
day); Hoover Dam Air Tour
(40 minutes); Red Rock Canyon
Air Tour (25 minutes).

Key Tours,
3305 West Spring Mountain Road,
Suite 92, Las Vegas, 89102.
(702) 362-9355. Tours depart
from the Four Queens, Silver City,
Flamingo Hilton, Circus Circus,
Excalibur and Tropicana hotels.

Hoover Dam (all day);
Laughlin Tour (all day).

**Lake Mead Air and Land/Air
Safaris,** *P.O. Box 60035, Boulder
City, 89006. Lake Mead Air
(702) 293-1848, 293-9906; Land/Air
Safaris (702) 384-1234, 293-1848,
(800) 634-6787.* Tours leave from
Boulder City office, 1601 Nevada
Highway.

Grand Canyon Air Tour
(90 minutes); Hoover Dam Land
Tour/Grand Canyon Air Tour (all
day)—Land tour portion by Gray
Line Tours. Hotel pickup.
Hoover Dam Air Tour (30 minutes); Hoover Dam/Lake Mead
Air Tour (one hour).

Ray and Ross Transport, Inc., *300 West Owens Avenue, Las Vegas, 89106. (702) 646-4661; (800) 338-8111 outside NV.* Hotel pickup. Infant's rate available. All tours are by motorcoach tours unless otherwise stated.

Grand Canyon Air and Ground Tour (all day); Grand Canyon Air Tour/Hoover Dam Ground Tour (all day); Hoover Dam Tour/Ethel M Chocolate Factory (all day); Hoover Dam/Lake Mead Cruise (all day); Hoover Dam/Mini City Tour (all day); Red Rock/Bonnie Springs Tour (all day); City Tour (all day); Mini City Tour (half day); Laughlin Tour (all day).

Scenic Airlines, *241 East Reno Avenue, Las Vegas, 89119; (702) 739-1900; (800) 634-6801 outside NV; FAX: (702) 739-8065.* Hotel pick-up. Children's rate available on some tours.

Grand Canyon (west end only) Highlights Air Tour (90 minutes); Grand Canyon Classic Air Tour (half day); Grand Canyon Explorer Fly and Hike Tour (all day); Grand Canyon Air and Ground Day Tour (all day); Grand Canyon Premium Deluxe Air and Ground Tour (all day); Grand Canyon Overnight Air Tour (one night); Grand Canyon Fly & Hike Overnight Tour (two nights); Monument Valley Discover Tour (all day); Monument Valley Grand Excursion (all day); Monument Valley (two days/one night, three days/two nights); Monument Valley (three days/two nights—Los Angeles); Bryce Canyon/Grand Canyon Tour (all day); Bryce Canyon/ Grand Canyon Deluxe Tour (all day); Bryce Canyon/Grand Canyon Overnight (one night); Best of the West—Bryce Canyon/Grand Canyon/ Monument Valley (three days/ two nights); Grand Medallion Premium Tour—Bryce Canyon/ Grand Canyon/Monument Valley (four days/three nights).

Sierra Nevada Airways, *P.O. Box 19398, Las Vegas, 89132-0398. (702) 736-6770.* Hotel pick-up. Children's rate available.

Grand Canyon Air Tour (half day); Grand Canyon Deluxe Air and Ground Tour (all day).

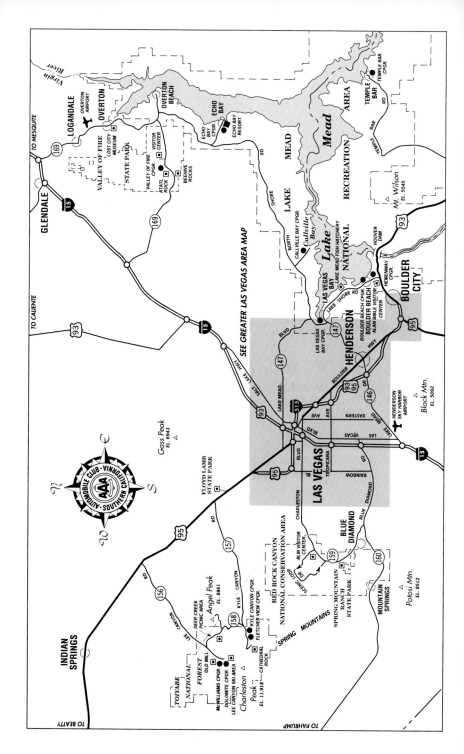

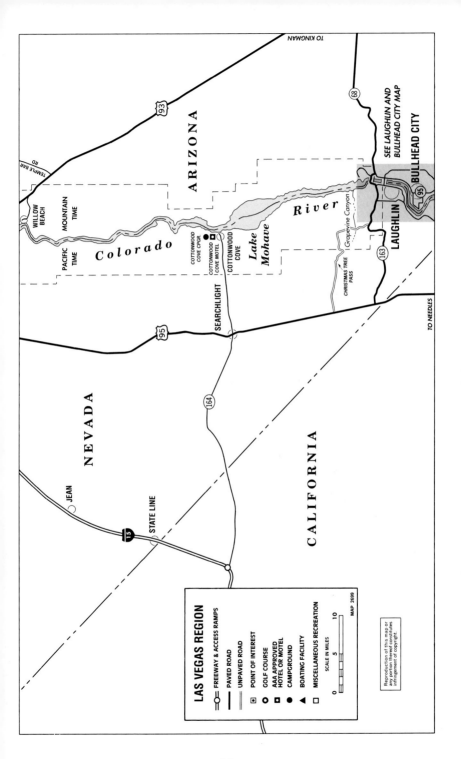

LAS VEGAS REGION

- ⊖ FREEWAY & ACCESS RAMPS
- — PAVED ROAD
- ═ UNPAVED ROAD
- ⊡ POINT OF INTEREST
- ○ GOLF COURSE
- ☐ AAA APPROVED HOTEL OR MOTEL
- ● CAMPGROUND
- ▲ BOATING FACILITY
- ☐ MISCELLANEOUS RECREATION

SCALE IN MILES

0   5   10

MAP 2699

Reproduction of this map or any portion thereof constitutes infringement of copyright.

61

ACTIVITIES FOR CHILDREN

Because Las Vegas is usually considered an adult-oriented city, visitors in the past have often left children at home. Today, however, Las Vegas itself and the surrounding areas offer many daytime diversions for the younger set. Some of the larger hotels have video arcades on the premises. Licensed babysitting services are also provided at all major hotels and at some smaller hotels; check with the hotel front desk. Additional child-care services can be found by referring to the Las Vegas telephone directory yellow pages under "Baby Sitters."

The Las Vegas Hilton Hotel operates a "youth hotel" for children and teen-agers ages 3 to 18. The cost is $4 per hour, per person. The facility is open to children of guests at either the Las Vegas Hilton or Flamingo Hilton hotels. The youth hotel, located in North Tower addition of the Las Vegas Hilton, contains five rooms which can accommodate a total of 120 youths at one time. Trained counselors supervise all activities, and food service is available. Hours during the summer months are 8 a.m. to midnight daily; winter hours are 10 a.m. to 10 p.m. Monday through Thursday, 10 a.m. to midnight Friday, 8 a.m. to midnight Saturday, and 8 a.m. to 10 p.m. Sunday. Parents may leave their children on an hourly basis with no advance notice required. There are also dormitories for overnight care during the summer and on Friday and Saturday nights during winter; dorm fee is $20 per night. Advance reservations are necessary for overnight use.

The MGM Grand Hotel operates a youth hotel with supervised activities for children of hotel guests. Details about King Looey's Youth Center were not available at press time. Call the hotel at (702) 891-7777 for more information.

The Circus Circus Hotel has several shops and food stands catering to children. There is also a second-floor, carnival-style arcade with numerous games of skill; most of the games cost from 50¢ to $1, and prizes are awarded to the winners. In addition, there are arcades with pinball and electronic games, and the hotel also presents free circus acts daily from 11 a.m. to midnight.

Grand Slam Canyon, adjacent to Circus Circus, is a five-acre climate-controlled indoor amusement park. The attractions include the nation's only double-loop, double-corkscrew indoor roller coaster. Hours are 10 a.m. to 10 p.m. daily. Admission is based on a point system; $10 is enough for one turn on each ride. An admission price of $3 is also available for those who just want to look, not ride.

The Excalibur Hotel features a medieval castle-theme exterior. The interior includes a Renaissance village with strolling performers, shops and carnival-style arcade

The Las Vegas Museum of Natural History has one of the most complete exhibits of animated dinosaur replicas in the Southwest.

games for children. Every night in King Arthur's Arena a jousting tournament is recreated with special effects and a cast of more than 30 performers. Excalibur also has a dynamic motion simulator called "Merlin's Magic Motion Machine" that provides filmed "rides" for passengers whose seats are programmed to move with the motion on the screen.

The mysteries of ancient Egypt are unveiled at the Luxor, a 30-story pyramid-shaped resort. The hotel features the "River Nile" flowing along the interior perimeter of the building, murals tracing 4000 years of Egyptian history, replicas of early Egyptian artifacts, a full-size reproduction of King Tut's tomb, and an entertainment complex featuring a video arcade and high-impact films that use motion simulators and large-screen film projections. The shows screen daily every 30 minutes beginning at 10 a.m. Admission is $5 per person.

Exciting amusement park rides can be found at MGM Grand Adventures, a 33-acre theme park at the MGM Grand Hotel. The park features roller coaster and water rides, bumper cars and a journey through a haunted mine, plus celebrity lookalikes, strolling performers and musical acts.

The Mirage Hotel has a spectacular five-story waterfall/volcano in front of the hotel, located virtually a stone's throw from the sidewalk on Las Vegas Boulevard. The volcano will fascinate adults as well as children as it erupts every 15 minutes. Dramatic lighting at night makes the waterfall appear to be flowing lava. Large crowds gather to watch, and traffic is often at a standstill, particularly at night; taking local transportation (such as a bus or shuttle) is recommended.

Animals are a popular Strip attraction. The Mirage has a glass-enclosed tiger habitat that offers 24-hour public viewing of Siegfried and Roy's beautiful Royal White tigers used in their stage show. The dolphin habitat at the Mirage features six Atlantic bottle-nosed dolphins. It is open from 11 a.m. to 7 p.m. Monday through Friday. Admission for ages 10 and over is $3. Future plans at Vegas World Hotel-Casino include a lion habitat.

Treasure Island's pirate shows and 18,000-square foot entertainment complex will provide hours of fun for children and adults alike. The entrance of the hotel is the spectacular Buccaneer Bay where hourly sea battles between a pirate ship and a British frigate take place. Mutiny Bay is the hotel's pirate-themed entertainment complex that features video games and pinball.

Other highlights for young people include visits to the Ethel M Chocolates Factory, Fashion Show shopping mall, Floyd Lamb State Park, Guinness World of Records Museum and Gift Shop, Hoover Dam, Imperial Palace Auto Collection, Kidd's Marshmallow Factory, Lake Mead National Recreation Area, Las Vegas Museum of Natural History, Lied Discovery Children's Museum, the Meadows Mall carousel, Red Rock Canyon recreation lands, Scandia Family Fun Center, Southern Nevada Zoological Park, Toiyabe National Forest, Valley of Fire State Park and Wet 'N Wild. Details about these attractions can be found in the *Points of Interest* section.

CAMPING

Warm weather and nearby scenic and recreation areas attract thousands of campers to the Las Vegas area every year. Camping accommodations range from simple RV lots located close to the gambling action and glitz to more rugged settings in the surrounding areas.

Campground listings are divided into two sections—Las Vegas and Surrounding Areas. Surrounding Areas include Lake Mead National Recreation Area, Toiyabe National Forest and Valley of Fire State Park.

The ⊛ emblem in a campground listing indicates the property is a AAA-approved facility and can display the AAA sign. A checkmark (√) after the name of the campground indicates that it is privately owned and has been inspected. State and federal campgrounds have not been inspected by AAA, but are listed as a convenience to members wishing to stay in these areas. Those campgrounds listed under **Other** may not meet all AAA standards but are listed as a service to members.

Each listing contains the total number of sites and the opening and closing dates. Rates quoted represent daily camping fees. Each listing includes the campground's location, mailing address and telephone number (if available), as well as a brief description. Unless otherwise noted, all campgrounds have drinking water, showers and flush toilets, and will accept pets on leashes.

Abbreviations are used as follows: (T) indicates number of sites for tent campers; (T/RV) indicates the number of interchangeable tent or recreational vehicle sites; (RV) indicates the number of sites exclusively for recreational vehicles. Electric, water and sewage hookups are designated by E, W and S; these are followed by the number of hookups available and any extra charges.

Many public campgrounds have limits on the number of consecutive days a visitor may stay. Travelers are advised to check directly with a campground regarding its stay limitations. Limits are usually as follows:

**Bureau of Land
Management (BLM)**   14 days

**County Parks
(County)**   14 days to no limit

**National Forests (NF)
State Forests (State)** 5 to 14 days

**National Parks and
Monuments (NPS)** 7, 14 or 30 days

State Parks (State)   14 days

Some private campgrounds in this area have 14-day stay limits for campers renting on a weekly basis. Many have monthly rates and sections of their RV parks that house "long term" residents. The rates and information for campgrounds listed are specifically for "overnight" camping or for those campers staying only a few days. For longer visits, arrangements should be made directly with the campground.

Reservations for some national forest campgrounds can be made by calling the National Forest Reservation Center at (800) 280-CAMP or TTD (800) 879-4496 (for the hearing/speech impaired). National Forest sites can be reserved up to 120 days prior to arrival; cancellation notice is 14 days. MasterCard, Visa and Discover cards are accepted. There is a non-refundable reservation fee of $7.50 for one family campsite, $15 for one group site. The cancellation fee is $7.50, plus additional penalties for no-show or late cancellations.

From January through September, the reservation center hours are Monday through Friday, 6 a.m. to 6 p.m.; Saturday and Sunday, 8 a.m. to 4 p.m. From October through December the hours are Monday through Friday only from 8 a.m. to 4 p.m.

Major credit cards honored by the campgrounds are abbreviated as follows: AE=American Express; DI=Diner's Club International; DS=Discover; MC=MasterCard; VI=Visa.

RV towing and tire-change service is available to Auto Club members for motorhomes, campers and travel/camping trailers. Information about these services is available at Auto Club offices.

LAS VEGAS
AAA Approved

Boulder Lakes
RV Resort (√)   417 sites   Open all year   AAA Special Value Rates
A/Y $16.50 for 2   XP $2   EWS-417
East of SR 93/95; exit Russell Rd, ¼ mi n at Desert Horizons Rd; 6201 Boulder Hwy, 89122. 10 acres. 50', RV-417. Desert atmosphere, paved roads & pads. Weekly & monthly rates available. Cable TV; phone hookups; flush toilets. Coin laundry. Groceries. 4 pools; saunas; whirlpools; putting green; recreation room. Credit card guarantee; 3-day refund notice. MC, VI. FAX (702) 435-1125.
                                                    (702) 435-1157

Circusland
RV Park (√)   370 sites   Open all year   Rates Subject to Change
Sun-Thu $12.96   EWS-370
Fri & Sat $17.28
2¾ mi s on the Strip; adjacent to Circus Circus Hotel at 500 Circus Circus Dr, 89109. 35 acres. RV-370. All paved sites; many pull-through sites. Flush toilets. Disposal station. Coin laundry. Groceries & propane. Pool; wading pool; sauna; whirlpool; playground. Pets. Reservation deposit required. AE, DS, MC, VI.
                                                    (702) 794-3757

Las Vegas
KOA (√)   300 sites   Open all year   Rates Subject to Change
A/Y $21.95 for 2   XP $3-$5   EW-240, $1; S-180, $2
4 mi se off US 93 & 95; ½ blk s off Desert Inn Rd at 4315 Boulder Hwy, 89121. 13 acres. T-60; RV-240. Many pull-through sites. A/C or heater, $3. Flush toilets. Disposal station. Coin laundry. Groceries & propane. 2 pools; wading pool; whirlpool; recreation room; sports court; playground. Pets. Credit card guarantee. AE, DS, MC, VI. FAX (702) 434-8729   (702) 451-5527

Nevada Palace VIP Travel
Trailer Park (√) 168 sites Open all year Rates Subject to Change
A/Y $9 EWS-168

7 mi se on US 93 & 95 at Sun Valley Dr; ½ mi n of Tropicana Ave at 5325 Boulder Hwy, 89122. 10 acres. RV-168. Pull-through sites; no tents allowed. Phone hookups. Flush toilets. Disposal station. Pool. 14-day stay limit. Reservation deposit required. DS, MC, VI. (702) 451-0232

Robert Brown

The dazzling lights of Fremont Street earned it the nickname Glitter Gulch.

Sam's Town
RV Parks (√) 500 sites Open all year Rates Subject to Change
⍟A/Y $12 EW-500, S-476

8 mi se on US 93, 95 & Nellis Blvd at 5225 Boulder Hwy, 89122. 22 acres. RV-500. No tents allowed. Some pull-through sites. Attractive grounds & facilities. Flush toilets. Disposal station. Coin laundry. 2 pools; whirlpools; recreation room. Pets. 14-day stay limit. Credit card guarantee. AE, DI, DS, MC, VI. **(See ad on page 87.)** (702) 454-8055

Other

The following establishments may not meet all AAA standards but are listed as a service.

California Hotel

RV Park   222 sites   Open all year   Rates Subject to Change
  A/Y $12   EWS-192; EW-30
Downtown at 1st St and Stewart Ave, 89101. RV-222. Flush toilets; hot showers. Disposal station. Coin laundry. Pool & whirlpool. Grocery store, ice. Small pets (fee), dog run. Reservations recommended. 24-hour refund notice. AE, MC, VI.
(800) 634-6505

Hacienda

Camperland   363 sites   Open all year   Rates Subject to Change
  6/1-9/30 $9.95 for 4   XP $1   EWS-363
  10/1-5/31 $14.95 for 4 XP $1
On the Strip, Las Vegas Blvd S, ½ mi s of Tropicana Ave; entrance is s of hotel, 89119. RV-363. Flush toilets; hot showers. Disposal station. Coin laundry. Pool; spa; tennis; playground. Picnic tables; grills. Pets $1. Reservation deposit required; 48-hour refund notice. AE, DS, MC, VI.
(702) 891-8243

Circus Circus Hotel/Casino

Las Vegas' warm weather and nearby scenic and recreation areas attract thousands of campers every year.

SURROUNDING AREAS
LAKE MEAD NATIONAL RECREATION AREA
Public

Boulder Beach   154 sites   Open all year   Rates Subject to Change
A/Y $8   EWS-80
6 mi ne of Boulder City off US 93, 89005. 33 acres. T/RV-100; RV-54. Hospital in Boulder City, 6 miles. Reservations not accepted. Restaurant. Boat ramp. Pets. 30-day stay limit. (NPS)   (702) 293-8906

Callville Bay   80 sites   Open all year   Rates Subject to Change
A/Y $8
26 mi ne of Boulder City on SR 167, Boulder City, 89005. 12 acres. T-70; RV-10. Hospital in Henderson, 25 miles. Reservations not accepted. No showers. Restaurant. Rental boats; boat ramp. Pets. 90-day stay limit. (NPS)   (702) 565-9612

Echo Bay   155 sites   Open all year   Rates Subject to Change
A/Y $8
30 mi s of Overton on SR 167, 89005. 11 acres. T-155. Hospital in Henderson, 50 miles. Reservations not accepted. No showers. Coin laundry & restaurant. Rental boats; boat ramp. Pets. 90-day stay limit. (NPS)
(702) 394-4060

Hemenway   184 sites   Open all year   Rates Subject to Change
A/Y $8
5 mi ne of Boulder City on SR 166, 89005. T/RV-184. Hospital in Boulder City, 6 mi. Reservations not accepted. No showers. Boat ramp. Pets. 30-day stay limit. (NPS)   (702) 293-8906

Las Vegas Bay   89 sites   Open all year   Rates Subject to Change
A/Y $8
15 mi n of Boulder City on SR 166, 89005. 12 acres. T-89. Hospital in Henderson, 10 miles. Reservations not accepted. No showers. Restaurant. Rental boats; boat ramp. Pets. 30-day stay limit. (NPS)   (702) 565-8368

Temple Bar   166 sites   Open all year   Rates Subject to Change
A/Y $8   EWS-14
54 mi e of Boulder City off US 93 and Temple Bar Rd; c/o 601 Nevada Hwy, Boulder City, 89005. T-153; RV-13. Hospital in Boulder City, 55 miles. Coin laundry. Restaurant. Swimming; rental boats; fishing. Reservations not accepted. No showers. Boat ramp. Pets. 90-day stay limit. (NPS)   (602) 767-3401

TOIYABE NATIONAL FOREST/
MOUNT CHARLESTON
Public

Dolomite   31 sites   Open 5/28-9/3   Rates Subject to Change
5/28-9/3 $8 for Fam
29 mi nw on US 95, 18 mi sw on SR 156, 89018. (8400'). 10 acres. T/RV-31. 20 units for reservation by calling (800) 280-CAMP. RV limit: 32'. Flush & vault toilets; no showers. Nature trails. Pets. 16-day stay limit. (NF)   (702) 873-8800

Fletcher View   12 sites   Open 5/26-9/3   Rates Subject to Change
5/26-9/3 $8 for Fam
5 mi nw on US 95, 18 mi w on SR 157, 89018. (7200'). 6 acres. T/RV-
12. RV limit: 22'. Vault toilets; no showers. 16-day stay limit. (NF)   (702) 873-8800

Kyle Canyon   25 sites   Open 5/15-10/15   Rates Subject to Change
5/15-10/15 $8 for Fam/$16 Multi-Fam
15 mi nw on US 95, 17½ mi w on SR 157, 89018. (7000'). 16 acres.
T/RV-25. RV limit: 32'. Vault toilets; no showers. 9 units for reservation by calling (800) 280-CAMP; 10 units are handicap accessible. 16-
day stay limit. (NF)   (702) 873-8800

McWilliams   31 sites   Open 5/1-9/30   Rates Subject to Change
5/1-9/30 $8
*29 mi nw on US 95, then 18 mi sw on SR 156; Las Vegas Ranger District, 550 E
Charleston, 89104.* (8400'). 10 acres. T/RV-31. 9 units for reservation by calling
(800) 280-CAMP. RV limit: 32'. Flush & vault toilets; no showers. 16-day stay
limit. (NF)   (702) 873-8800

VALLEY OF FIRE STATE PARK
Public

Valley of Fire
State Park   50 sites   Open all year   Rates Subject to Change
A/Y $4
50 mi ne of Las Vegas via I-15 and SR 169; c/o Box 515, Overton, 89040. T/RV-
50. Attendant. 38,480 acres. Disposal station. Flush & vault toilets; cold showers. Nature trails; visitor center. Pets on leash. (State)   (702) 397-2088

LODGING AND RESTAURANTS

When choosing accommodations from the more than 86,000 rooms avail-
able in Las Vegas, remember that it is important to make reservations as
far in advance as possible. "No vacancy"' signs are constant reminders
that the town operates at near capacity all year. During peak periods, a
one-night reservation for Friday or Saturday night is difficult to obtain.
Remember also, that most resort hotels do not confirm advance reserva-
tions at a definite rate. When making reservations, be sure to ask the
amount of deposit required and the refund policy. Auto Club members
can make hotel and motel reservations at their nearest district office.

*T*here are several things to be considered in addition to price when staying in Las Vegas. It is easier to obtain reservations to sell-out celebrity shows if you stay at the hotel where the performer is appearing. If easy access to your car is important, staying at a motel would be more convenient than a hotel. Golf privileges, tennis and spa facilities may also be a consideration.

Dining in Las Vegas is as varied as accommodations. Prices range from less than $1 for breakfast to more than $50 for gourmet dinners. All of the large hotels have several places to eat, and many have theme dining rooms that feature regional or ethnic decor and food. Many coffee shops are open 24 hours a day. Buffets are available at almost every major hotel and offer diners a choice of three or four entrees, plus potatoes, vegetables, salads, desserts and a beverage for one price; buffet-style champagne brunches are offered at numerous hotels on weekends. A list of AAA-approved restaurants follows the hotel and motel listings.

The lodging and restaurant properties listed in these pages have been inspected at least once in the past year by a trained representative of the Automobile Club of Southern California. In surprise inspections, each property was found to meet AAA's extensive and detailed requirements for approval. These requirements are reflective of current industry standards and the expectations of the traveling public. Less than two-thirds of the lodging establishments open for business are listed in AAA publications.

Virtually all listings include AAA's esteemed "Diamond" rating, reflecting the overall quality of the establishment. Many factors are considered in the process of determining the Diamond rating. In lodging properties, the facility is first "classified" according to its physical design—is it a motel, a hotel, a resort, an apartment, etc. Since the various types of lodging establishments offer differing amenities and facilities, rating criteria are specific for each classification. For example, a motel, which typically offers a room with convenient parking and little if any recreational or public facilities, is rated using criteria designed only for motel-type establishments—it is not compared to a hotel with its extensive public and meeting areas, or to a resort with its wide range of recreational facilities and programs. The diamonds do, however, represent standard levels of quality in all types of establishments.

There is no charge for a property to be listed in AAA publications. Many lodgings and restaurants, however, choose to advertise their AAA approval by displaying the ⊕ emblem on the premises and using it in their advertising. These properties are especially interested in serving AAA members.

Properties are listed alphabetically under the nearest town, with lodging facilities first and restaurants second. The location is given from the center of town or from the nearest major highway.

Nearly all lodging and restaurant facilities accept credit cards as forms of payment for services rendered. The following symbols are used to identify the specific cards accepted by each property.

AE	American Express
CB	Carte Blanche
DI	Diner's Club International
DS	Discovery
ER	En Route (European)
JCB	Japanese Credit Bureau
MC	MasterCard
VI	VISA

Some lodgings and restaurants listed in Auto Club publications have symbols indicating that they are accessible to individuals with disabilities. The criteria used in qualifying these listings are consistent with, but do not represent the full scope of, the Americans with Disabilities Act of 1990. AAA does not evaluate recreational facilities, banquet rooms or convention and meeting facilities for accessibility. Individuals with disabilities are urged to phone ahead to fully understand an establishment's facilities and accessibility.

In accommodations, a [⟨⟩] indicates that at least one fully accessible guest room exists and that an individual with mobility impairments will be able to park and enter the building, register, and use at least one food and beverage outlet. For restaurants, the symbol indicates that parking, dining rooms and rest rooms are accessible.

The [⟨⟩] at the end of a lodging listing means that the following elements are provided: closed captioned decoders; text telephones; visual notification for fire alarms, incoming phone calls and door knocks; and phone amplification devices.

LODGING

The following accommodations classifications appear in this book.

Bed & Breakfast—Usually a small establishment emphasizing personal attention. Individually decorated guest rooms provide an at-home feeling and may lack some amenities such as TVs, phones, etc. Usually owner-operated with a common room or parlor where guests and owners can interact during evening and breakfast hours. May have shared bathrooms. A continental or full hot breakfast is included in the room rate.

Complex—A combination of two or more kinds of lodgings.

Cottage—Individual bungalow, cabin or villa, usually containing one rental unit equipped for housekeeping. May have a separate living room and bedroom(s). Parking is usually at each unit.

Country Inn—Similar in definition to a bed and breakfast. Offers a dining room reflecting the ambience of the inn. At a minimum, breakfast and dinner are served.

Hotel—A multi-story building usually including a coffee shop, dining room, lounge, room service, convenience shops, valet, laundry and full banquet/meeting facilities. Parking may be limited.

Lodge—Typically two or more stories with all facilities in one building. Located in vacation, ski, fishing areas, etc. Usually has food and beverage service. Adequate on-premises parking.

Motel—Usually one or two stories; food service, if any, consists of a limited facility or snack bar. Often has a pool or playground. Ample parking, usually at the guest room door.

Motor Inn—Usually two or three stories, but may be a high-rise. Generally has recreation facilities, food service and ample parking. May have limited banquet/meeting facilities.

Apartment—Usually four or more stories with at least half the units equipped for housekeeping. Often in a vacation destination area. Units typically provide a full kitchen, living room and one or more bedrooms, but may be studio-type rooms with kitchen equipment in an alcove. May require minimum stay and/or offer discounts for longer stays. This classification may also modify any of the other lodging types.

Condominium—A destination property located in a resort area. Guest units consist of a bedroom, living room and kitchen. Kitchens are separate from bedrooms and are equipped with a stove, oven or microwave, refrigerator, cooking utensils and table settings for the maximum number of people occupying the unit. Linens and maid service are provided at least twice weekly. This classification may also modify any of the other lodging types.

Historic—Accommodations in restored, pre-1930 structures, reflecting the ambience of yesteryear and the surrounding region. Rooms may lack some modern amenities and have shared baths. Usually owner-operated and provides food service. Parking is usually available. This classification may also modify any of the other lodging types.

Resort—May be a destination unto itself. Has a vacation atmosphere offering extensive recreational facilities for such specific interests as golf, tennis, fishing, etc. Rates may include meals under American or Modified American plans. This classification may also modify any of the other lodging types.

Suite—Units have one or more bedrooms and a living room, which may or may not be closed off from the bedrooms. This classification may also modify any of the other lodging types.

A property's **diamond rating** is not based on the room rate or any one specific aspect of its facilities or operations. Many factors are considered in calculating the rating, and certain minimum standards must be met in all inspection categories. If a property fails approval in just one category, it is not listed in Club publications. The inspection categories include housekeeping, maintenance, service, furnishings and decor.

Guest comments received by AAA may also be reviewed in a property's approval/rating process.

These criteria apply to all properties listed in this publication:

- Clean and well-maintained facilities
- Hospitable staff
- Adequate parking
- A well-kept appearance
- Good quality bedding and comfortable beds with adequate illumination
- Good locks on all doors and windows
- Comfortable furnishings and decor
- Smoke detectors
- Adequate towels and supplies
- At least one comfortable easy chair with adequate illumination
- A desk or other writing surface with adequate illumination

Lodging ratings range from one to five diamonds and are defined below:

◆—Good but unpretentious. Establishments are functional. Clean and comfortable rooms must meet the basic needs of privacy and cleanliness.

◆◆—Shows noticeable enhancements in decor and/or quality of furnishings over those at the one-diamond level. May be recently constructed or an older property. Targets the needs of a budget-oriented traveler.

◆◆◆—Offers a degree of sophistication with additional amenities, services and facilities. There is a marked upgrade in services and comfort.

◆◆◆◆—Excellent properties displaying high levels of service and hospitality and offering a wide variety of amenities and upscale facilities, inside the room, on the grounds and in the common areas.

◆◆◆◆◆—Renowned for an exceptionally high degree of service, striking and luxurious facilities and many extra amenities. Guest services are executed and presented in a flawless manner. Guests are pampered by a very professional, attentive staff. The property's facilities and operations set standards in hospitality and service.

Occasionally a property is listed without a rating, such as when an establishment is under construction or renovations are in progress and a rating cannot be determined.

Room rates shown in the listings are provided by each establishment's management for publication by the Auto Club. During special events or holiday periods rates may exceed those published and special discounts or savings programs may not be honored. High-season rates are always shown; off-season rates are listed if they are substantially lower than the rest of the year. Rates are for typical rooms, not special units, and do not include taxes. When a property submits its rates, it also indicates which of three *rate options* is to be listed. Listings stating *Rates Subject to Change* mean that the published rates may be changed by the establishment during the life of the publication. The two other rate options are available only to AAA members who identify themselves as such upon registration and request the listed rate option. Where a listing says *Guaranteed, Rates* the management has agreed to honor the published rates for AAA members. The third rate option, *AAA Special Value Rates*, gives AAA members at least 10 percent off the published rates. Some properties offer discounts to senior citizens, or special rate periods such as weekly or monthly rentals.

Inquiries as to the availability of any special discounts should be made at the time of registration. Typically, a property will allow guests to take advantage of only one discount during their stay (i.e., a guest staying at a property offering both the *AAA Special Value Rates* and Senior Discount may choose only one of the two savings plans).

Each rate line gives the dates for which the rates are valid, and the rates for one person (abbreviated 1P), two persons with one bed (2P/1B), two persons with two beds (2P/2B), and the rate for each extra person (XP) not included in the family rate. Figures following these abbreviations are the price(s) for the specified room and occupants. Most rates listed are European plan, which means that no meals are included in the rate. Some lodgings' rates include breakfast [BP] or continental breakfast [CP]. A few properties offer the American Plan [AP] which includes three meals, or a Modified American Plan [MAP] which offers two meals, usually breakfast and dinner.

All baths have a combination tub and shower bath unless noted otherwise. Since nearly all establishments have air conditioning, telephones and color TV, only the absence of any of these items is noted in the listing. Check in time is shown only if it is after 3 p.m.; check out time is shown only if it is before 10 a.m. Service charges are not shown unless they are $1 or more, or at least 5 percent of the room rate. If the pet acceptance policy varies within the establishment, no mention of

pets is made. By U.S. and Canada laws, pet restrictions do not apply to guide dogs. A heated pool is heated when it is reasonable to expect use of a pool. Outdoor pools may not open in winter.

Reservations are always advisable in resort areas and may be the only way to assure obtaining the type of accommodations you want.

Deposits are almost always required. Should your plans change and you need to cancel your reservation, be aware of the amount of notice required to receive a refund of your deposit.

Many properties welcome children in the same room with their parents at no additional charge; individual listings indicate if there is an age limit. There may be charges for additional equipment, such as roll-aways or cribs. Some properties offer a discount for guests ages 60 and older—be aware that the Senior Discount cannot usually be taken in conjunction with or in addition to other discounts.

Fire warning and protection equipment are indicated by the symbols D (all guest rooms have smoke detectors) and S (all guest rooms have sprinklers). Many properties have reserved rooms for non-smokers; look for the ⊘ symbol in the listing and be sure to request a non-smoker room both when you make a reservation and upon registration.

RESTAURANTS

Restaurants listed in this publication have been found to be consistently good dining establishments. In metropolitan areas, where many restaurants are above average, we select some of those known for the superiority of their food, service and atmosphere and also those offering a selection of quality food at moderate prices (including some cafeterias and family restaurants). In smaller communities the restaurants considered to be the best in the area may be listed.

The type of cuisine featured at a restaurant is used as a means of classification for restaurants. You will find listings for Steakhouses and Continental cuisine as well as a range of ethnic foods, such as Chinese, Japanese, Italian and yes, American. Special menu types, such as early bird, a la carte, children's or Sunday Brunch, are also listed. We have tried to indicate something about each restaurant's atmosphere and appropriate attire. The availability of alcoholic beverages is shown, as well as entertainment and dancing.

Price ranges for an average, complete meal without alcoholic beverage are indicated by each $ symbol representing 10-dollar increments in the price range. Taxes and tips are not included.

Restaurant ratings are applied to two categories of operational style—full-service eating establishments, and self-service, family-dining operations such as cafeterias or buffets.

◆—Good but unpretentious dishes. Table settings are usually simple and may include paper placemats and napkins. Alcoholic beverage service, if any, may be limited to beer and wine. Usually informal with an atmosphere conducive to family dining.

◆◆—More extensive menus representing more complex food preparation and, usually, a wider variety of alcoholic beverages. The atmosphere is appealing and suitable for either family or adult dining. Service may be casual, but host or hostess seating can be expected. Table settings may include tablecloths and cloth napkins.

◆◆◆—Extensive or specialized menus and a more complex cuisine preparation requiring a professional chef contribute to either a formal dining experience or a special family meal. Cloth table linens, above-average quality table settings, a skilled service staff and an inviting decor should all be provided. Generally, the wine list includes representatives of the best domestic and foreign wine-producing regions.

◆◆◆◆—An appealing ambience is often enhanced by fresh flowers and fine furnishing. The overall sophistication and formal atmosphere visually create a dining experience more for adults than for families. A wine steward presents an extensive list of the best wines. Smartly attired, highly skilled staff is capable of describing how any dish is prepared. Elegant silverware, china and correct glassware are typical. The menu includes creative dishes prepared from fresh ingredients by a chef who frequently has international training. Eye-appealing desserts are offered at tableside.

◆◆◆◆◆—A world-class operation with even more luxury and sophistication than four-diamond restaurants. A proportionally large staff, expert in preparing tableside delicacies, provides flawless service. Tables are set with impeccable linens, silver and crystal glassware.

LODGING
LAS VEGAS

Alexis Park Resort Hotel
Resort Hotel ◆◆◆
(702) 796-3300; FAX (702) 796-4334   *Guaranteed Rates*

All Year	1P 85.00-585.00	2P/1B 85.00-585.00	2P/2B 85.00-585.00 XP 15

I-15 exit e Tropicana Ave; 2 blks w of UNLV; 2 mi s of Convention Center at 375 E Harmon Ave (89109). Check in 4 pm. 500 rooms; many with gas fireplaces. Spacious landscaped grounds. 12 two-bedroom, two-story suites, $335-$1150 for up to 4 persons; 2 stories; exterior corridors; business center; meeting rooms. Bars; free & pay movies; refrigerators; cable TV. Some coffee makers, whirlpools. Putting green; 3 pools; saunas; 2 lighted tennis courts. Fee for massage. Data ports; PC; secretarial services. Senior discount. $50 non-refundable deposit required. AE, CB, DI, DS, MC, VI. Restaurant; coffee shop; 6 am-midnight, $12-$80; cocktails & lounge; 24-hour room service; entertainment. Ⓓ Ⓢ ⊘

Arizona Charlie's Hotel ⒶⒶⒶ
Motor Inn ◆◆
(702) 258-5111; FAX (702) 258-5197   *Rates Subject to Change*

Fri & Sat	1P 45.00	2P/1B 45.00	2P/2B 45.00 XP 4
Sun-Thu	1P 28.00	2P/1B 28.00	2P/2B 28.00 XP 4

1 mi nw of I-15; Charleston Blvd exit; 740 S Decatur Blvd at Evergreen Ave (89107). 100 rooms. Old West atmosphere. 3 stories; interior corridors. Pool; bowling. Valet laundry. Airport transportation. No pets. Children 12 & under stay free. Reservation deposit required. AE, DI, DS, MC, VI. Coffee shop; 24 hours; $7-$11; buffet, $5; casino; cocktails & lounge. Ⓚ Ⓓ Ⓢ ⊘

Bally's Casino Resort-Las Vegas ⒶⒶⒶ
Hotel ◆◆◆
(702) 739-4111; FAX (702) 739-4405   *Rates Subject to Change*

All Year	1P $86.00-180.00	2P/1B 86.00-180.00	2P/2B 86.00-180.00 XP 15

4½ mi s on the Strip at 3645 Las Vegas Blvd S (Box 96505, 89109). 2832 rooms. Rooms in two towers connected by casino & public areas. 3-bedroom units, 1- & 2-bedroom suites & penthouses, $256-1500 for 2 persons. 26 stories; interior corridors; conference facilities; convention oriented; meeting rooms; luxury level rooms. Cable TV; pay movies; some refrigerators. Pool; sauna; steamroom; whirlpool; 10 lighted tennis courts. Fee for health club, massage. Data ports; valet parking. No pets. Children 18 & under stay free; package plans. Reservation deposit required. AE DI, DS, JCB, MC, VI. 4 restaurants, 2 coffee shops; 24 hours; $8-34; buffet, $12; 4:30-10 pm; cocktails & lounge; casino; name entertainment. Ⓓ Ⓢ ⊘

Barbary Coast Hotel
Hotel ◆◆◆
(702) 737-7111; FAX (702) 737-6304   *Rates Subject to Change*

Fri & Sat	1P 75.00	2P/1B 75.00	2P/2B 75.00 XP 5
Sun-Thu	1P 50.00	2P/1B 50.00	2P/2B 50.00 XP 5

1¾ mi s on the Strip at 3595 Las Vegas Blvd S (Box 19030, 89132). 200 rooms; Gay 90s decor, including large tiffany-style stained glass mural. 12 suites $150-$350 for up to 2 persons. 8 stories; interior corridors. Free & pay movies; cable TV; some refrigerators, whirlpools, roll-in showers. Data ports. No pets. Reservation deposit required. AE, CB, DI, DS, MC, VI. Restaurant; coffee shop; 24 hours; $7-$20; casino; cocktails. 🖋 Ⓓ Ⓢ ⊘

Barcelona Motel ⓐⓐ

(702) 644-6300; FAX (702) 644-6510

				Motor Inn ◆

Rates Subject to Change

Fri & Sat	1P 50.00	2P/1B 55.00	2P/2B 55.00	XP 5
Sun-Thu	1P 35.00	2P/1B 42.50	2P/2B 42.50	XP 5

7 mi ne; ½ mi from Nellis AFB; I-15 exit 48 via Craig Rd at 5011 E Craig Rd (89115). 179 rooms; comfortable rooms. 2 stories; exterior corridors. Pay movies; some shower baths, refrigerators; kitchens; no utensils; fee for safes. Coin laundry. Pool; whirlpool. No pets. Senior discount. Reservation deposit required. AE, DI, DS, MC, VI. Coffee shop; 24 hours; $6-$10; small casino; cocktails; entertainment. Ⓓ ⊘

Best Western Main Street Inn ⓐⓐ

(702) 382-3455; FAX (702) 382-1428

Motor Inn ◆◆

Rates Subject to Change

Fri & Sat	1P 50.00-58.00	2P/1B...	2P/2B 55.00-60.00	XP 7
Sun-Thu 6/1-8/4	1P 40.00-48.00	2P/1B...	2P/2B 45.00-50.00	XP 7
Sun-Thu 2/1-5/31				
& 8/5-1/31	1P 39.00-44.00	2P/1B...	2P/2B 44.00-46.00	XP 7

I-15N, exit 43E; I-15S, exit 44E; 1000 N. Main St (89101). 91 rooms; near downtown convention center. 2-3 stories; exterior corridors; meeting rooms. Pool; some refrigerators. Coin laundry. Pets, $7. Senior discount. Reservation deposit required. AE, DI, DS, MC, VI. Restaurant; 24 hours; $8-$12; cocktail lounge. Ⓓ ⊘

Best Western Mardi Gras Inn ⓐⓐ

(702) 731-2020; FAX (702) 733-6994

Motor Inn ◆◆

AAA Special Value Rates

12/28-12/31	1P 80.00-90.00	2P/1B 80.00-90.00	2P/2B 86.00-96.00	XP 6
1/1-5/31 &				
9/1-11/30	1P 40.00-50.00	2P/1B 40.00-50.00	2P/2B 46.00-56.00	XP 6
6/1-8/31	1P 36.00-46.00	2P/1B 40.00-50.00	2P/2B 40.00-50.00	XP 6
12/1-12/27	1P 36.00-46.00	2P/1B 36.00-46.00	2P/2B 36.00-46.00	XP 6

½ mi s of convention center at 3500 Paradise Rd (89109). 314 rooms; 3 stories; exterior corridors; meeting rooms. Free & pay movies; cable TV; refrigerators; some coffee makers. Pool; whirlpool. Coin laundry. Phone charge $1.50 per day added. Airport transportation. No pets. Children 12 & under stay free; senior discount. AE, CB, DI, DS, ER, JCB, MC, VI. Restaurant; 7 am-10 pm; $9-$14; cocktails. Ⓓ

Best Western Nellis Motor Inn ⓐⓐ

(702) 643-6111; FAX (702) 643-8553

Motel ◆◆

Rates Subject to Change

Fri & Sat 5/25-9/3	1P 49.00	2P/1B 55.00	2P/2B 55.00	XP 6
Fri & Sat 9/4-5/24	1P 45.00	2P/1B 51.00	2P/2B 51.00	XP 6
Sun-Thu 5/25-9/3	1P 39.00	2P/1B 45.00	2P/2B 45.00	XP 6
Sun-Thu 9/4-5/24	1P 37.00	2P/1B 43.00	2P/2B 43.00	XP 6

7 mi ne; ¼ mi from Nellis AFB; exit I-15, exit 48E at 5330 E. Craig Rd (89115). 52 rooms; comfortable rooms; attractive decor. 2 stories; exterior corridors; Free & pay movies; cable TV; rental VCPs. Pool; playground. Coin laundry. Pets: Dogs only-$50 deposit and $6 daily. Children 12 & under stay free; Senior discount. Reservation deposit required. AE, DI, DS, JCB, MC, VI. Coffee shop nearby. Ⓓ ⊘

Best Western Parkview Inn ⓐⓐ

(702) 385-1213

Motel ◆◆

Rates Subject to Change

Fri & Sat	1P 48.00	2P/1B 52.00	2P/2B 58.00	XP 6
Sun-Thu 5/27-8/29	1P 40.00	2P/1B 42.00	2P/2B 50.00	XP 6
Sun-Thu 2/1-5/26				
& 8/30-1/31	1P 38.00	2P/1B 42.00	2P/2B 46.00	XP 6

8 blks n on US 91 & 93 at 905 Las Vegas Blvd N (89101). 56 rooms; across from city park. 2 stories; exterior corridors. Pool. Coin laundry. Pets, $6 daily. Children 12 & under stay free. Senior discount. Reservation deposit required; 14-day notice. AE, CB, DI, DS, MC, VI. Ⓓ ⊘

Blair House Hotel 🏵

Apartment Motel ♦♦

(702) 792-2222; FAX (702) 792-9042

Rates Subject to Change

Fri & Sat [CP]	1P 85.00	2P/1B 85.00	2P/2B 85.00	XP 10
Sun-Thu [CP]	1P 65.00	2P/1B 65.00	2P/2B 65.00	XP 10

Exit I-15 at Sahara to the Strip; 344 E. Desert Inn Rd (89109). 224 rooms; residential atmosphere. 3 stories; exterior corridors. Kitchens; cable TV; pay movies; rental VCPs. Pool; whirlpool. Coin laundry. No pets. Children 18 & under stay free. Senior discount. Reservation deposit required. AE, DI, DS, MC, VI. Ⓓ Ⓢ ⊘

Boardwalk Hotel-Casino

Motor Inn ♦

(702) 735-1167; FAX (702) 739-8152

Rates Subject to Change

All Year	1P 45.00-90.00	2P/1B 45.00-90.00	2P/2B 45.00-90.00 XP 6

4¾ mi s on the Strip at 3750 Las Vegas Blvd S (89109). 2-night minimum stay on holidays; 201 rooms; many units set back from the Strip. 4-6 stories; interior corridors. Cable TV; pay movies; some radios. 2 pools. Coin laundry. Pets, $10 plus $50 deposit. AE, DI, DS, ER, MC, VI. 2 coffee shops; 24 hours; $5-$11; casino; cocktails. Ⓓ ⊘

Caesars Palace 🏵

Hotel ♦♦♦♦

(702) 731-7110; FAX (702) 731-6636

Rates Subject to Change

All Year	1P 95.00-160.00	2P/1B 110.00-175.00	2P/2B 120.00-175.00 XP 20

4½ mi s on the Strip, I-15 exit E Flamingo Rd; 3570 Las Vegas Blvd S (89109). 3- night minimum stay on major holidays. 1515 rooms; attractively landscaped grounds & marble statuary; large rooms. The forum shops' common areas resemble Roman streetscapes; elegant shopping mall, art galleries & eateries. 2-23 stories; interior corridors; business center; conference facilities; meeting rooms. Free movies; cable TV; some shower baths; some refrigerators, safes, whirlpools. 2 pools (1 heated); sauna; whirlpool; 4 tennis courts (2 lighted). Fee for health club & massage. Secretarial services. No pets. 24-hour room service. Package plans. Reservation deposit required. AE, CB, DI, DS, JCB, MC, VI. 7 restaurants; coffee shop; $10-$60; buffet; $12; casino; cocktail lounge; name entertainment. Ⓓ Ⓢ ⊘

California Hotel

Hotel ♦♦

(702) 385-1222; FAX (702) 388-2660

Rates Subject to Change

Fri & Sat	1P 50.00	2P/1B 50.00	2P/2B 50.00	XP 5
Sun-Thu	1P 40.00	2P/1B 40.00	2P/2B 40.00	XP 5

In downtown casino center area at 1st & Ogden (Box 630, 89125). 635 rooms; "Aloha"-style decor. 11-13 stories; interior corridors; meeting rooms. Safes; some refrigerators. Swimming pool & whirlpool open 4/1-10/31. Recreation program. Valet parking. No pets. Reservation deposit required. AE, CB, DI, DS, MC, VI. 2 restaurants; coffee shop; 24 hours; casino; $8-$25; cocktails & lounge. Ⓓ Ⓢ

Carriage House 🏵

Apartment Hotel ♦♦

(702) 798-1020; FAX (702) 798-1020

Rates Subject to Change

All Year	1P 85.00-190.00	2P/1B 85.00-190.00	2P/2B 85.00-190.00

1 blk e off the Strip at 105 E Harmon Ave (89109). 143 rooms; attractively decorated. 15 two-bedroom units, $190-$245 for 2-8 persons. 9 stories; interior corridors. Free movies; cable TV; some shower baths. Some efficiencies, kitchens, microwaves, coffee makers. Pool; whirlpool; 1 lighted tennis court. Fee for safes & VCPs. Coin laundry. Area transportation to Strip and convention center; airport transportation. No pets. Children stay free. Senior discount. Reservation deposit required. AE, DI, DS, ER, MC, VI. Restaurant; 7 am-10 am & 5:30 pm-11 pm; $9-$16; cocktails. Ⓓ Ⓢ ⊘

Casino Royale and Hotel

Motel ◆◆◆

(702) 737-3500; FAX (702) 737-1973

Fri & Sat	1P 69.00	2P/1B 69.00	2P/2B 69.00	XP 10
Sun-Thu	1P 35.00	2P/1B 35.00	2P/2B 35.00	XP 10

4 mi s on the Strip at 3419 Las Vegas Blvd S (89109). 160 rooms. Formerly Center Strip Travelodge. 4 stories; interior corridors. Pool. Pay movies. No pets. Credit card guarantee. AE, MC, VI. Casino; restaurant nearby. Ⓓ ⊘

Center Strip Inn

Motel ◆

(702) 739-6066; FAX (702) 736-2521

Fri & Sat	1P 49.95-69.95	2P/1B 59.95-79.95	2P/2B 59.95-79.95	XP 10
Sun-Thu	1P 29.95-39.95	2P/1B 39.95-59.95	2P/2B 39.95-59.95	XP 10

4½ mi s on the Strip at 3688 Las Vegas Blvd S (89109). 105 rooms. 17 two-bedroom units; spa/steam rooms, $69-$99 Sun-Thu; $89-$109 Fri & Sat. Deluxe spa suites, $99-$129 Sun-Thu; $109-$149 Fri & Sat. 2-5 stories; exterior corridors; meeting rooms. Free movies. Some microwaves, radios, steambaths, whirlpools. Coin laundry. Pool. No pets. Reservation deposit required. AE, CB, DI, DS, ER, MC, VI. Coffee shop nearby. Ⓓ ⊘

Circus Circus Hotel

Hotel ◆◆

(702) 734-0410; FAX (702) 734-5897

All Year	1P 21.00-65.00	2P/1B 21.00-65.00	2P/2B 21.00-65.00

2¾ mi s on the Strip at 2880 Las Vegas Blvd S (Box 14967, 89114). 2793 rooms; featuring amusement park with raft slide, roller coaster & motion machines in an environmentally-controlled dome. Circus entertainment 11 am to midnight. Maximum rates for up to 4 persons. 2-29 stories; interior corridors. Some shower baths; roll-in showers; some refrigerators. 3 pools; whirlpool. Data ports. Valet parking. No pets. Children 12 & under stay free. Reservation deposit required. AE, CB, DI, DS, MC, VI. 3 restaurants; 2 coffee shops; 24 hours; $5-$18; buffet, $4; casino; cocktails.
🅟 Ⓓ Ⓢ ⊘

Comfort Inn South ⏧

Motel ◆◆

(702) 736-3600; FAX (702) 736-0726

Fri & Sat [CP]	1P 58.00	2P/1B 65.00	2P/2B 65.00	XP 5
Sun-Thu [CP]	1P 38.00	2P/1B 42.00	2P/2B 42.00	XP 5

½ mi e of I-15; Tropicana Ave exit; 5075 S Koval Ln (89109). 106 rooms; comfortable rooms. 2 stories; exterior corridors; meeting rooms. Free movies; cable TV. Pool. Valet laundry. No pets. Children 18 & under stay free. Senior discount. Reservation deposit required. AE, DI, DS, ER, JCB, MC, VI. Ⓓ ⊘

Courtyard by Marriott

Motor Inn ◆◆◆

(702) 791-3600; FAX (702) 796-7981

All Year	1P 82.00	2P/1B 92.00	2P/2B 92.00

3 blks e off the Strip; 1 blk to convention center; 3275 Paradise Rd (89109). 149 rooms; attractively decorated. 3 stories; interior corridors; meeting rooms. Free & pay movies; coffee makers. Pool; whirlpool; exercise room. Fee for refrigerators. Coin laundry. Airport transportation. No pets. AE, CB, DI, DS, MC, VI. Restaurant; 6:30 am-2 pm & 5-10 pm; $8-$16; cocktails. Ⓓ Ⓢ ⊘

Days Inn-Downtown ⏧

Motel ◆

(702) 388-1400; FAX (702) 388-9622

Fri & Sat	1P 50.00-100.00	2P/1B 60.00-100.00	2P/2B 60.00-100.00	XP 10
Sun-Thu	1P 36.00-100.00	2P/1B 46.00-100.00	2P/2B 46.00-100.00	XP 10

On US 93 & 95 business rt; 707 E Fremont St (89101). 146 rooms; 3 stories; exterior corridors. 7 one-bedroom suites, $60-$110. Cable TV; rental VCPs. No pets. Children 12 & under stay free. Senior discount. Credit card guarantee. AE, CB, DI, DS, JCB, MC, VI. Coffee shop; 24 hours; $5-$8; slot casino; cocktails. Ⓓ ⊘

Econo Lodge

Motel ◆

(702) 382-6001; FAX (702) 382-9180

AAA Special Value Rates

All Year   1P 40.00-50.00   2P/1B 40.00-55.00   2P/2B 70.00

Exit I-15 e at Charleston Ave s on the Strip; between the Strip & downtown casino areas at 1150 Las Vegas Blvd S (89104). 123 rooms; 2 stories; exterior corridors. Some kitchens, VCPs; no utensils. Pool. Pets. Credit card guarantee. Ⓓ ⊘

Econo Lodge-Downtown

Motel ◆

(702) 384-8211; FAX (702) 384-8580

Rates Subject to Change

Fri & Sat	1P 45.00	2P/1B 45.00	2P/2B 50.00	XP 5
Sun-Thu	1P 35.00	2P/1B 35.00	2P/2B 40.00	XP 5

Exit I-15 downtown casino center at 520 S Casino Center Blvd (89101). 3-night minimum stay on major holidays. 48 rooms; near downtown casinos. 3 stories; interior corridors; 4 one-bedroom apartments, $69-$95 for up to 4 persons. Refrigerators; some coffee makers, kitchens, no utensils. Coin laundry. No pets. Children 18 & under stay free. Senior discount. Reservation deposit required. 3-day refund notice. AE, CB, DI, DS, JCB, MC, VI. Ⓓ ⊘

Excalibur Hotel & Casino

Hotel ◆◆◆

(702) 597-7777; FAX (702) 597-7009

Rates Subject to Change

Fri & Sat	1P 65.00-79.00	2P/1B 65.00-79.00	2P/2B 65.00-79.00	XP 7
Sun-Thu	1P 39.00-52.00	2P/1B 39.00-52.00	2P/2B 39.00-52.00	XP 7

I-15 exit e Tropicana Ave at 3850 Las Vegas Blvd S (Box 96778, 89193). 4032 rooms; medieval castle theme. 28 stories; interior corridors; conference facilities; meeting rooms. Shower baths. Pay movies. Fee for refrigerators, whirlpools. Valet laundry. Valet parking. 2 pools. No pets. Children 12 & under stay free. Reservation deposit required. AE, CB, DI, DS, MC, VI. Dining room; 5 restaurants; coffee shop; 24 hours; $5-$30; buffet, $5; casino; cocktails & lounge; 24-hour room service; entertainment. Ⓓ Ⓢ ⊘

Fairfield Inn by Marriott

Motel ◆◆

(702) 791-0899; FAX (702) 791-0899

Rates Subject to Change

9/1-1/31	1P 50.95	2P/1B 56.95	2P/2B 56.95	XP 3
2/1-6/1	1P 47.95	2P/1B 53.95	2P/2B 53.95	XP 3
6/2-8/31	1P 43.95	2P/1B 49.95	2P/2B 49.95	XP 3

I-15 exit e Flamingo Rd; 3 blks n of convention center at 3850 Paradise Rd (89109). 129 rooms. Large lobby with many tables & chairs; comfortable rooms. 4 stories; interior corridors; meeting rooms. Free movies; cable TV. Pool; whirlpool. No pets. Airport transportation. AE, DI, DS, MC, VI. Restaurant nearby. Ⓓ Ⓢ ⊘

Flamingo Hilton-Las Vegas

Hotel

(702) 733-3111; FAX (702) 733-3528

Rates Subject to Change

All Year   1P 72.00-139.00   2P/1B 72.00-139.00   2P/2B 72.00-139.00   XP 16

I-15 exit e Flamingo Rd, n on the Strip at 3555 Las Vegas Blvd S (89109). Under major renovation. Rating withheld pending completion of new construction & remodeling. 3527 rooms. Many large rooms. 2-28 stories; interior corridors; conference facilities; meeting rooms. Pay movies; some safes. 2 pools; whirlpool; 4 lighted tennis courts. Fee for health club, massage, refrigerators. Valet laundry. Valet parking; No pets. Children 14 & under stay free. Credit card guarantee; 3-day refund notice. AE, DI, DS, MC, VI. 5 restaurants; cafeteria; coffee shop; 24 hours; $7-$20; buffet, $5-$8; casino; cocktails & lounge; 24-hour room service; entertainment. **(See ad on next page.)** Ⓓ Ⓢ ⊘

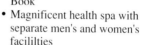
Four Queens Hotel 🅐🅐🅐

Hotel ♦♦

(702) 385-4011; FAX (702) 383-0631

Rates Subject to Change

Fri & Sat

5/29-9/28 1P 57.00	2P/1B 57.00	2P/2B 57.00	XP 8
Sun-Thu 1P 47.00	2P/1B 47.00	2P/2B 47.00	XP 8

In the downtown casino center area at 202 E. Fremont St (89101). Check in 4 pm. 709 rooms; comfortable rooms. 38 suites, $85-$95 for up to 2 persons. 18 stories; interior corridors; meeting rooms. Pay movies; some shower baths; some safes. Valet laundry. Valet parking. No pets. Senior discount. Reservation deposit required. AE, DI, DS, MC, VI. Restaurant; coffee shop; 24-hours; $7-$29; casino; cocktails; 24-hour room service; entertainment. Ⓓ Ⓢ ⊘

Gold Coast Hotel

Hotel ♦♦♦

(702) 367-7111; (702) 367-8575

Guaranteed Rates

Fri & Sat 1P 50.00	2P/1B 50.00	2P/2B 50.00	
Sun-Thu 1P 35.00	2P/1B 35.00	2P/2B 35.00	

1 blk w of I-15, exit Flamingo Rd W; 4000 W Flamingo Rd (Box 80750, 89180). 722 rooms; Colonial-Spanish architecture. 18 suites with wet bars & refrigerators, $100-$150 for 2 persons. 10 stories; interior corridors; conference facilities. Free & pay movies; cable TV; some bars; fee for refrigerators. Valet parking. Pool; whirlpool; bowling; movie theaters. No pets. Credit card guarantee. AE, CB, DI, DS, ER, JCB, MC, VI. Dining room; restaurant; coffee shop; 24 hours; $5-$17; buffet, $6; casino; cocktails & lounge; 24-hour room service; entertainment. Ⓓ Ⓢ ⊘

Golden Nugget Hotel 🏅   **Hotel**   ◆◆◆◆

(702) 385-7111; FAX (702) 386-8362   *AAA Special Value Rates*

All Year   1P 58.00-150.00   2P/1B 58.00-150.00   2P/2B 58.00-150.00   XP 12

In the downtown casino center area at 129 E. Fremont St (Box 2016, 89101). 1907 rooms. One & two bedroom suites, $210-$300 for 2 persons. 10-22 stories; interior corridors; conference facilities; meeting rooms. Attractive contemporary decor; large rooms. Cable TV. Pool; whirlpool. Fee for health club. Video arcade. Valet laundry. Massage. Valet parking. No pets. Children 12 & under stay free; Reservation deposit required. AE, DI, DS, MC, VI. 2 dining rooms; restaurant; coffee shop; 24 hours; $10-$35; buffet, $10; 24-hour room service; casino; cocktails & lounge; entertainment. 🅰 Ⓓ Ⓢ ⊘

Harrah's-Las Vegas   **Hotel**   ◆◆◆

(702) 369-5000; FAX (702) 369-6014   *Rates Subject to Change*

Fri & Sat 2/21-5/29 & 9/2-11/12 1P 95.00-120.00	2P/1B 95.00-120.00	2P/2B 95.00-120.00	XP 10
Fri & Sat 5/30-9/1 & 11/13-2/20 1P 92.00-118.00	2P/1B 92.00-118.00	2P/2B 92.00-118.00	XP 10
Sun-Thu 2/21-5/29 & 9/2-11/12 1P 75.00-100.00	2P/1B 75.00-100.00	2P/2B 75.00-100.00	XP 10
Sun-Thu 5/30-9/1 & 11/13-2/20 1P 62.00- 88.00	2P/1B: 62.00- 88.00	2P/2B 62.00- 88.00	XP 10

4 mi s on the Strip at 3475 Las Vegas Blvd S (89109). 3-night minimum stay on major holidays. 1709 rooms; 15-35 stories. 64 suites, $175-$350 for up to 2 persons. Interior corridors; conference facilities; meeting rooms. Free & pay movies; cable TV. Pool; whirlpool. Coin laundry. Fee for massage & health club. Valet parking. No pets. Children 14 & under stay free. Senior discount. Package plans. Reservation deposit required. AE, CB, DI, DS, ER, JCB, MC, VI. 4 restaurants; coffee shop; 24 hours; $9-$29; buffet, $6; cocktails & lounge; entertainment. Ⓓ Ⓢ ⊘

Holiday Inn 🏅   **Motor Inn**   ◆◆◆

(702) 732-9100; FAX (702) 731-9784   *AAA Special Value Rates*

All Year [CP]   1P 59.00-175.00   2P/1B 59.00-175.00   2P/2B 59.00-175.00   XP 15

I-15 exit e Flamingo Rd at 325 E Flamingo Rd (89109). Formerly Emerald Springs Inn. 150 rooms; attractive public areas & rooms. 3 stories; interior corridors. Suites, $99-$250 for up to 2 persons. Conference facilities; meeting rooms. Free & pay movies; refrigerators; cable TV; some coffee makers. Fee for VCPs. Pool; whirlpool; exercise room. Secretarial services. Valet laundry. Area transportation to Strip-24 hours; airport transportation. No pets. Children 18 & under stay free. Senior discount. Age restrictions may apply. AE, DI, DS, MC, VI. Restaurant; 6:30 am-2:30 pm & 10 pm; Fri & Sat to 11 pm; $10-$20; cocktails & lounge. Ⓓ Ⓢ ⊘

Lady Luck Casino & Hotel 🏅   **Hotel**   ◆◆

(702) 477-3000; FAX (702) 384-2832   *Rates Subject to Change*

All Year   1P 39.00-75.00   2P/1B 39.00-75.00   2P/2B 39.00-75.00   XP 8

3rd & Ogden at 206 N. 3rd St. (Box 1060, 89125). 791 rooms. Few poolside units. 2-25 stories. 165 suites with whirlpool bath, $50-$90 for 2 persons. Interior corridors. Cable TV; pay movies; some refrigerators. Pool. Valet laundry. Valet parking. Airport transportation. No pets. Package plans. Reservation deposit required. AE, DI, DS, JCB, MC, VI. Dining room; 2 restaurants; coffee shop; 24-hours; $7-$24; buffet, $5; casino; cocktails & lounge. Ⓓ Ⓢ ⊘

La Quinta Motor Inn ⓐ
Motel ◆◆

(702) 739-7457; FAX (702) 736-1129 *Rates Subject to Change*

Fri & Sat	1P 59.00-66.00	2P/1B 67.00-74.00	2P/2B 67.00	XP 8
Sun-Thu	1P 49.00-56.00	2P/1B 57.00-64.00	2P/2B 57.00	XP 8

5½ mi s on the Strip at 3782 Las Vegas Blvd S (89109). 114 rooms. Spanish exterior design. 3 stories; exterior corridors. Free & pay movies; cable TV. Airport transportation. Small pets only. AE, CB, DI, DS, MC, VI. Coffee shop nearby. Ⓓ ⊘

Las Vegas Hilton ⓐ
Hotel ◆◆◆◆

(702) 732-5111; FAX (702) 732-5249 *Rates Subject to Change*

All Year	1P 85.00-180.00	2P/1B 85.00-180.00	2P/2B 85.00-180.00	XP 25

4 blks e off the Strip; adjacent to convention center at 3000 Paradise Rd (Box 93147, 89193). 3174 rooms; 30 stories. 300 suites, $290-$950 for up to 2 persons. Interior corridors; business center; conference facilities; convention oriented; meeting rooms; luxury level rooms. Safes; cable TV; pay movies; some refrigerators, steambaths. Putting green; pool; whirlpool; 6 lighted tennis courts. Health club; playground. Massage. Data ports; PCs; secretarial services. Valet laundry. Valet parking. No pets. Credit card guarantee; 3-day refund notice. AE, CB, DI, DS, MC, VI. Dining room; coffee shop; 12 restaurants; 24 hours; buffet, $7-$10; restaurant, $8-$35; cocktails; 24-hour room service; also *Benihana Village*, see separate listing; name entertainment. Ⓓ Ⓢ ⊘

Luxor Las Vegas
Resort Hotel

(702) 795-8118 *Guaranteed Rates*

Fri & Sat	1P 79.00-99.00	2P/1B 79.00-99.00	2P/2B 79.00-99.00	XP 10
Sun-Thu	1P 49.00-79.00	2P/1B 49.00-79.00	2P/2B 49.00-79.00	XP 10

I-15 exit e Tropicana, just s on the Strip at 3900 Las Vegas Blvd S (89119). Too new to rate, rating withheld pending inspection. Egyptian pyramid design. 2526 rooms; 30 stories; interior corridors. Cable TV. Pool; sauna; whirlpool. Valet parking. No pets. Children 12 & under stay free. AE, CB, DI, DS, MC, VI. 7 restaurants; cocktail lounge; 24-hour room service. Ⓓ Ⓢ

MGM Grand Hotel Casino & Theme Park
Resort Hotel

(702) 891-7777; FAX (702) 891-1030 *Rates Subject to Change*

All Year	1P 59.00-129.00	2P/1B 59.00-129.00	2P/2B 59.00-129.00	XP 10

I-15 exit e Tropicana Ave; 3799 Las Vegas Blvd S (89109). Too new to rate, rating withheld pending inspection. 5014 rooms. World's largest hotel; 33-acre theme park. 400 suites, $150-$1500 up to 2 persons. 30 stories; interior corridors; business center; conference facilities; meeting rooms. Cable TV. Heated pool; 5 lighted tennis courts. Fee for massage. Secretarial services. Valet laundry. Valet parking. No pets. Children 12 & under stay free. Reservation deposit required. AE, CB, DI, DS, JCB, MC, VI. 5 restaurants; coffee shop; $10-$30; buffet, $7; casino. Ⓓ Ⓢ ⊘

The Mirage ⓐ
Resort Hotel ◆◆◆◆

(702) 791-7111; FAX (702) 791-7446 *Rates Subject to Change*

Fri & Sat	1P 99.00-279.00	2P/1B 99.00-279.00	2P/2B 99.00-279.00	XP 15
Sun-Thu	1P 69.00-279.00	2P/1B 69.00-279.00	2P/2B 69.00-279.00	XP 15

3½ mi s on the Strip at 3400 Las Vegas Blvd S (Box 9193, 89109). 3044 rooms. Lavish grounds & unique public areas; home to Siegfried & Roy & their magnificent white tigers. 1 & 2 bedroom suites, $300-$750 for 2 persons. 30 stories; interior corridors; business center; conference facilities; meeting rooms; luxury level rooms. Free movies; cable TV. Some refrigerators, safes, steambaths. Putting green; 2 heated pools; wading pool; whirlpools. Fee for 18 holes golf, massage. Health club. Data ports; PCs; secretarial services. Valet parking. No pets. Children 12 & under stay free. Package plans. Reservation deposit required. AE, CB, DI, DS, JCB, MC, VI. Dining room; 7 restaurants; coffee shop; 24 hours; $6-$50; buffet, $6.50-$9.50; Sun, $12.50; 24-hour casino; cocktails & lounge; name entertainment. Ⓓ Ⓢ ⊘

Plaza Suite Hotel by Howard Johnson

(702) 369-4400; FAX (702) 369-3770

Motor Inn ◆◆◆
Rates Subject to Change

9/1-11/15 &				
12/28-6/14	1P 95.00-125.00	2P/1B 95.00-125.00	2P/2B 125.00	XP 15
6/15-8/31	1P 65.00- 75.00	2P/1B 65.00- 75.00	2P/2B 75.00	XP 15
11/16-12/27	1P 55.00- 65.00	2P/1B 55.00- 65.00	2P/2B 65.00	XP 15

Exit I-15 Flamingo, e ½ mi to Paradise, s ¼ mi to 4255 S Paradise Rd (89109). 202 rooms. Atrium lobby, vibrant colors, cascading waterfall. 6 stories; interior corridors; conference facilities; meeting rooms. Free & pay movies; cable TV; refrigerators; some coffee makers. Pool; sauna; whirlpool; exercise room. Secretarial services. Valet laundry. Area transportation to Strip & convention center; airport transportation. Pets. Children 18 & under stay free. Reservation deposit required. AE, DI, DS, ER, JCB, MC, VI. Restaurant; 6 am-midnight; $8-$16; cocktails. Ⓓ Ⓢ ⊘

Residence Inn by Marriott

(702) 796-9300; FAX (702) 796-9562

Apartment Hotel ◆◆◆
Rates Subject to Change

All Year [CP] 1P 95.00-149.00	2P/1B 95.00-149.00	2P/2B 135.00-199.00

Opposite convention center at 3225 Paradise Rd (89109). Check in 4 pm; 192 rooms. 48 two-bedroom units; maximum rates for up to 4 persons. 2 stories; exterior corridors; meeting rooms. Kitchens; free movies; cable TV. Heated pool; whirlpools; sports court. Coin laundry. Airport transportation. Pets. Children stay free. Senior discount. Credit card guarantee. AE, CB, DI, DS, JCB, MC, VI. Complimentary snacks & beverages 5:30 pm-7 pm weekdays. Ⓓ Ⓢ ⊘

Rio Suite Hotel & Casino ⓐⓐⓐ

(702) 252-7777; FAX (702) 252-8909

Hotel ◆◆◆
Rates Subject to Change

Fri & Sat	1P 101.00-150.00	2P/1B 101.00-150.00	2P/2B 101.00-150.00 XP 15
Sun-Thu	1P 85.00-101.00	2P/1B 85.00-101.00	2P/2B 85.00-101.00 XP 15

Exit I-15 at Flamingo Rd; ¼ mi w to 3700 W Flamingo Rd (Box 14160, 89103). 860 rooms. Large rooms. Attractive decor. Sand beach at pool. Specialty suites, $300-$850. 20 stories; interior corridors; meeting rooms. Refrigerators; safes; cable TV; pay movies. Some roll-in showers, coffee makers. Heated pool; whirlpool. Valet laundry. Valet parking. No pets. Children 12 & under stay free. AE, CB, DI, MC, VI. Dining room; 4 restaurants; coffee shop; 24 hours; $8-$22; buffet, $7; casino; 24-hour room service; cocktails; entertainment. Ⓓ Ⓢ ⊘

Riviera Hotel

(702) 734-5110; (702) 794-9451

Hotel ◆◆◆
Rates Subject to Change

All Year	1P 59.00-95.00	2P/1B 59.00-95.00	2P/2B 59.00-95.00 XP 12

2¾ mi s on the Strip at 2901 Las Vegas Blvd S (89109). 2200 rooms. Many large rooms; wedding chapel. 6-24 stories; interior corridors; business center; conference facilities; convention oriented; meeting rooms. Safes; cable TV; pay movies. Some radios; refrigerators. Pool; whirlpool; 2 lighted tennis courts. Fee for health club, massage. Secretarial services. Valet parking. No pets. Children 11 & under stay free. Package plans. Reservation deposit required. AE, CB, DI, DS, JCB, MC, VI. 3 restaurants; coffee shop; 24 hours; $7-$35; buffet, $5-$7; casino; cocktails & lounge; entertainment. Ⓓ Ⓢ

Rodeway Inn ⓐⓐⓐ

(702) 736-1434; FAX (702) 736-6058

Motel ◆
AAA Special Value Rates

Fri & Sat	1P 69.00	2P/1B 69.00	2P/2B 69.00
Sun-Thu	1P 49.00	2P/1B 49.00	2P/2B 49.00

5½ mi s on the Strip at 3786 Las Vegas Blvd S (89109). 2-night minimum stay on major holidays. 97 rooms. Few units overlooking golf course. Across from MGM Hotel & Theme Park. 5 two-bedroom units; 2-bedroom family units & 2 special rooms, $75-$150 for up to 6 persons. 2 stories; exterior corridors; meeting rooms. Free movies; cable TV; some coffee makers. Pool. Pets, $10. Children 18 & under stay free. Senior discount. AE, CB, DI, DS, ER, JCB, MC, VI. Coffee shop nearby. Ⓓ ⊘

St. Tropez All Suites Hotel

Complex ◆◆◆

(702) 369-5400; FAX (702) 369-1150 *Rates Subject to Change*
All Year [CP] 1P 93.00-140.00   2P/1B 93.00-140.00   2P/2B 119.00-140.00 XP 12
2 mi s of convention center at Paradise Rd; 455 E. Harmon Ave (89109). 149 rooms. Attractive landscaped grounds; courtyard units with patio or deck. Whirlpool units, $104-$160 for up to 2 persons. 2 stories; interior/exterior corridors; meeting rooms. Bars; safes; some shower baths; cable TV; VCPs. Some coffee makers. Pool; whirlpool; exercise room. Fee for movies. Airport transportation. No pets. Children 12 & under stay free. Senior discount. Reservation deposit required. AE, DI, DS, MC, VI. Complimentary evening beverages. Cocktail lounge; restaurant nearby. Ⓓ ⊘

Sam's Town Hotel

Hotel ◆◆

(702) 456-7777; FAX (702) 454-8014 *Rates Subject to Change*
All Year   1P 45.00   2P/1B 45.00   2P/2B 45.00   XP 5
On US 93 & 95 at Nellis Blvd; 5111 Boulder Hwy (89122). 197 rooms. Old West atmosphere; modern rooms. 3 stories; interior corridors. Pool; bowling. Valet parking. No pets. Children 12 & under stay free. Credit card guarantee. AE, DI, DS, MC, VI. 3 restaurants; coffee shop; 24 hours; $6-$18; buffet, $7; casino; cocktails & lounge. **(See ad on next page.)** Ⓓ ⊘

Sheffield Inn ⊛

Apartment Motel ◆◆

(702) 796-9000; FAX (702) 796-9000 *Rates Subject to Change*
All Year [CP] 1P 98.00   2P/1B 98.00   2P/2B 98.00
¾ mi s of convention center, exit I-15 Flamingo Ave e; ½ mile e of the Strip; 3970 Paradise Rd (89109). Check in 4 pm. 228 rooms; some units with balconies; few with patios. Large grassy areas. 9 two-bedroom units; maximum rates for up to 6 persons. 42 one-bedroom units, $125; 9 two-bedroom units, $200. 3 stories; interior corridors; meeting rooms. Free movies; safes; cable TV. Some efficiencies, kitchens, coffee makers. Pool; whirlpool. Coin laundry. Airport transportation. No pets. Children stay free. Senior discount. Package plans. Reservation deposit required. AE, CB, DI, DS, ER, MC, VI. Cafeteria, 11:30 am-10:30 pm; $10-$18. Ⓓ ⊘

Sheraton Desert Inn ⊛

Resort Complex ◆◆◆◆

(702) 733-4444; FAX (702) 733-4774 *Rates Subject to Change*
9/1-5/31   1P 90.00-175.00   2P/1B 90.00-175.00   2P/2B 90.00-175.00 XP 15
6/1-8/31   1P 75.00-150.00   2P/1B 75.00-150.00   2P/2B 75.00-150.00 XP 15
On the Strip, I-15 northbound exit e Flamingo Ave, southbound exit e Sahara Ave; 3145 Las Vegas Blvd S (89109). 821 rooms. Attractive landscaped grounds. 95 two-bedroom units. 2-14 stories; interior corridors; conference facilities; meeting rooms. Refrigerators; cable TV; pay movies. Heated pool; sauna; whirlpool; spa; 10 lighted tennis courts; jogging. Valet laundry. Valet parking. Fee 18 holes golf. Health club. No pets. Package plans. Reservation deposit required. A Preferred Hotel. AE, DI, DS, JCB, MC, VI. Dining room; 2 restaurants; coffee shop; 24 hours; $8-$34; casino; 24-hour room service; cocktails; name entertainment. Ⓓ ⊘

Somerset House Motel ⊛

Motel ◆◆

(702) 735-4411; FAX (702) 369-2388 *Rates Subject to Change*
Fri & Sat   1P 33.00   2P/1B 45.00   2P/2B 45.00   XP 3
Sun-Thu   1P 28.00   2P/1B 36.00   2P/2B 36.00   XP 3
3 mi s, 1 blk e off the Strip. 1 blk from convention center at 294 Convention Center Dr (89109). 104 rooms; some rooms with balcony. Free movies; refrigerators; cable TV. Some efficiencies, kitchens, roll-in showers. Pool. Coin laundry. Children 12 & under stay free. Senior discount. Weekly & monthly rates available. AE, CB, DI, MC, VI. Ⓓ ⊘

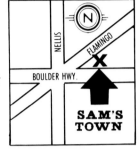
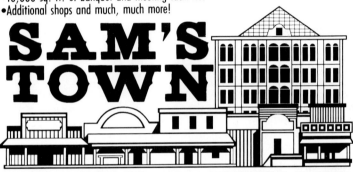
Treasure Island at the Mirage

Resort Hotel

(702) 894-7111

Rates Subject to Change

Fri & Sat	1P 75.00-189.00	2P/1B 75.00-189.00	2P/2B 75.00-189.00 XP 10
Sun-Thu	1P 45.00- 99.00	2P/1B 45.00- 99.00	2P/2B 45.00- 99.00 XP 10

3½ mi s on the Strip at 3300 Las Vegas Blvd S (Box 7711, 89193). Too new to rate, rating withheld pending inspection. 2900 rooms. Pirate-themed resort; home to Cirque du Soleil. 36 stories; interior corridors; conference facilities; meeting rooms. 212 one-bedroom suites, $100-$500 for up to 2 persons. Cable TV; some shower baths. Putting green; pool; whirlpool; arcade. Fee for 18 holes golf, massage. Health club. Data ports; secretarial services; PC. Valet laundry. Valet parking. No pets. Children 12 & under stay free. Package plans. Reservation deposit required. AE, CB, DI, DS, JCB, MC, VI. 2 dining rooms; 6 restaurants; coffee shop; $6-$30; 3 theme buffets, $6-$12; cocktails & lounge; name entertainment. Ⓓ Ⓢ ⊘

Tropicana Hotel   **Hotel**   ◆◆◆
(702) 739-2222; FAX (702) 739-2469   *Rates Subject to Change*

Fri & Sat	1P 129.00	2P/1B 129.00	2P/2B 129.00	XP 10
Sun-Thu	1P 55.00-99.00	2P/1B 55.00-99.00	2P/2B 55.00-99.00	XP 10

Exit I-15 Tropicana e; 3801 Las Vegas Blvd S (Box 97777, 89193). 1910 rooms. Tropical landscaping, pools, ponds & waterfalls. Tower & garden rooms. 120 suites, $225 for up to 2 persons. 22 stories; interior corridors; conference facilities; meeting rooms; luxury level rooms. Safes; cable TV; pay movies; some radios; rental refrigerators. Fee for saunas. Health club. 3 pools (1 indoor/outdoor); whirlpools. Valet laundry. Valet parking. No pets. Children 18 & under stay free. Reservation deposit required. 5 restaurants; 2 coffee shops; 24 hours; $6-$32; Fri & Sat buffet, $6; casino; cocktails & lounge; 24-hour room service; entertainment. Ⓓ Ⓢ ⊘

Union Plaza Hotel 🆔   **Hotel**   ◆◆
(702) 386-2110; FAX (702) 382-8281   *Rates Subject to Change*

All Year	1P 50.00	2P/1B 50.00	2P/2B 50.00	XP 8

Adjacent to casino center at 1 Main St (Box 760, 89125). 1037 rooms; large rooms. 22-25 stories; interior corridors; conference facilities; meeting rooms. Some refrigerators. 4 lighted tennis courts; jogging. Coin laundry. Valet parking. No pets. Reservation deposit required. AE, DI, DS. 2 restaurants; coffee shop; 24 hours; $6-$15; casino; cocktails; 24-hour room service; entertainment. Ⓓ Ⓢ ⊘

SURROUNDING AREAS
BOULDER CITY

Best Western Lighthouse Inn 🆔   **Motel**   ◆◆◆
(702) 293-6444; FAX (702) 293-6547   *AAA Special Value Rates*

Fri & Sat [CP]	1P 68.00	2P/1B 68.00	2P/2B 68.00
Sun-Thu [CP]	1P 58.00	2P/1B 58.00	2P/2B 58.00

1 mi e via SR 93 at 110 Ville Dr (89005). 70 rooms. Some rooms with view of Lake Mead. 3 stories; exterior corridors. Coffee makers; free movies; cable TV. Pool; whirlpool. Coin laundry. No pets. Children 12 & under stay free. Reservation deposit required. AE, DI, DS, MC, VI. Ⓓ Ⓢ ⊘

El Rancho Boulder Motel 🆔   **Motel**   ◆◆
(702) 293-1085   *Guaranteed Rates*

All Year	1P 50.00-65.00	2P/1B 50.00-65.00	2P/2B 60.00-90.00	XP 10

On US 93 at 725 Nevada Hwy (89005). 39 rooms. Spanish style. Attractive landscaped grounds. 9 two-bedroom units. 2 stories; exterior corridors. Free movies; cable TV; refrigerators. Pool. No pets. Reservation deposit required; 7-day refund notice. AE, DI, DS, MC, VI. Coffee shop nearby. Ⓓ ⊘

Sands Motel 🆔   **Motel**   ◆
(702) 293-2589   *Rates Subject to Change*

All Year	1P 32.00-38.00	2P/1B 38.00-44.00	2P/2B 40.00-48.00	XP 6

On US 93 at 809 Nevada Hwy (89005). 25 rooms. Some small units. 2 two-bedroom units. Exterior corridors. Cable TV; free movies; refrigerators; some shower baths. No pets. Reservation deposit required; 3-day refund notice. AE, DI, DS, MC, VI. Ⓓ ⊘

HENDERSON

Best Western Lake Mead Motel 🆔   **Motel**   ◆◆
(702) 564-1712; FAX (702) 564-7642   *Rates Subject to Change*

All Year	1P 37.00-51.00	2P/1B 42.00-56.00	2P/2B 42.00-56.00	XP 5

On SR 146; ½ mi w off Boulder Hwy, US 93 & 95. 85 W Lake Mead Dr (89015). 58 rooms. Comfortable rooms. Attractive decor. 2 stories; exterior corridors. Coffee makers; some refrigerators; free movies; cable TV. Pool. Coin laundry. No pets. Children 12 & under stay free. Reservation deposit required. AE, DI, DS, MC, VI. Ⓓ ⊘

JEAN

Primadonna Resort & Casino 🅰️🅰️
(702) 382-1212; FAX (702) 874-1749
Fri & Sat   1P 31.00   2P/1B 31.00
Sun-Thu   1P 18.00   2P/1B 18.00

Motor Inn   ◆◆
Rates Subject to Change
2P/2B 31.00
2P/2B 18.00

East of & adjacent to I-15, State Line exit; 45 mi s of Las Vegas. P.O. Box 95997, Las Vegas (89193). 2-night minimum stay on Fri & Sat. 661 rooms. Ferris wheel, carousel & monorail. 4 stories; interior corridors; meeting rooms. Cable TV; pay movies. Fee for whirlpools. Putting green; pool; whirlpool; playground. Valet parking. No pets. AE, DI, DS, MC, VI. Restaurant, coffee shop; 24 hours; $5-$14; cocktails & lounge; entertainment. **(See ad below.)** Ⓓ Ⓢ ⊘

Whiskey Pete's Hotel & Casino
(702) 382-4388; FAX (702) 874-1554
Fri & Sat   1P 31.00   2P/1B 31.00
Sun-Thu   1P 18.00   2P/1B 18.00

Hotel   ◆◆
Rates Subject to Change
2P/2B 31.00   XP 5
2P/2B 18.00   XP 5

West of & adjacent to I-15, State Line exit; 45 mi s of Las Vegas. P.O. Box 93718, Las Vegas (89193-3718). 2-night minimum stay on Fri & Sat. 726 rooms. 2-20 stories; interior corridors. Cable TV; pay movies. Pool; wading pool; whirlpool. Valet parking. No pets. Children 16 & under stay free. AE, CB, DI, DS, MC, VI. Restaurant, coffee shop; 24 hours; $5-$14; buffet, $3.80; casino; cocktails; entertainment. Ⓓ Ⓢ ⊘

LAKE MEAD-ECHO BAY

Echo Bay Resort 🅰️🅰️
(702) 394-4000; FAX (702) 394-4182
All Year   1P 69.00   2P/1B 74.00

Motor Inn   ◆
Rates Subject to Change
2P/2B 69.00-84.00   XP 6

On Lake Mead; 4 mi e of SR 169. Lake Mead. (Overton, 89040). 3-night minimum stay on holidays. 52 rooms. Some rooms with lake view; many with balcony or patio. 4 family rooms, $84 for up to 4 persons. 2 stories; interior corridors; meeting rooms. Cable TV; pay movies. Coin laundry. Marina; fishing, waterskiing; houseboats. Rental boats. Pets, $5 plus $25 refundable deposit. Reservation deposit required. MC, VI. Restaurant; 7 am-8:30 pm; 5/1-9/30; 6 am-9:30 pm; $8-$17; cocktails & lounge. Ⓓ

RESTAURANTS
LAS VEGAS

Alpine Village Inn Ⓐ *German* **$$** ◆
(702) 734-6888
Opposite Las Vegas Hilton at 3003 Paradise Rd (89109). European atmosphere. Swiss & American dishes. Children's menu; Rathskeller serves a la carte items. Cocktails & lounge; imported & domestic beer & wine; minimum charge $5. Reservations suggested. Valet parking. Open 5-11 pm. AE, DI, DS, MC, VI. ⊘

Andre's Ⓐ *French* **$$$$** ◆◆◆
(702) 385-5016
At Lewis St; 401 S 6th St (89101). Country-French decor; several dining rooms. A la carte. Cocktails & lounge. Reservations suggested. Valet parking. Open 6-11 pm. AE, MC, VI. ⊘

Battista's Hole in the Wall *Italian* **$$** ◆
(702) 732-1424
I-15 exit Flamingo Rd e ¼ mi, 1 blk e of the Strip; 4041 Audrie (89109). Rustic decor; casual atmosphere. Children's menu. Cocktails & lounge. Dinners include wine & cappuccino; minimum charge $6. Reservations suggested. Open 5-11 pm. AE, CB, DI, MC, VI. Closed 11/28, 5/27 & three weeks at Christmas.

Benihana Village *Ethnic* **$$$** ◆◆
(702) 732-5801
In Las Vegas Hilton at 3000 Paradise Rd (89114). Japanese village atmosphere including running streams & rain storms. Hibachi & Robata Yaki style cooking. Children's menu. Cocktails & lounge. Entertainment. Reservations suggested. Open 6-11 pm. AE, CB, DI, MC, VI.

Country Inn *American* **$$** ◆◆
(702) 731-5035
2 mi e of the Strip at 2425 E Desert Inn Rd (89121). Attractive country decor; casual atmosphere; casual dress. Children's menu. A la carte. Beer & wine only. Open 7 am-10 pm; Fri & Sat to 11 pm. AE, CB, DI, MC, VI. Closed 12/25. ⊘

Country Inn *American* **$$** ◆◆
(702) 254-0520
Exit I-15 Charleston, 4 mi w; s Rainbow, ¼ mi; 1401 S. Rainbow (89102). Attractive country decor, traditional dishes, friendly atmosphere; casual dress. Children's menu. A la carte. Beer & wine only. Open 7 am-10 pm; Fri & Sat to 11 pm. AE, CB, DI, MC, VI. Closed 12/25. ⊘

Famous Pacific Fish Co. *Seafood* **$$** ◆◆
(702) 796-9676
Exit I-15, Flamingo e 1 mi; ½ mi n to 3925 S Paradise Rd (89109). Attractive fish house decor, casual lively atmosphere; casual dress. Children's menu. Cocktails & lounge. Reservations suggested. Open 11 am-10 pm; Fri & Sat to 11 pm. AE, CB, DI, MC, VI. Closed 11/24 & 12/25. ⊘

Golden Steer   *Steakhouse*   **$$$**   ◆◆

(702) 384-4470

Exit I-15 Sahara, ¼ mi e; 1 blk w of the Strip at 308 W Sahara Ave (89102). Quiet atmosphere; semi-formal attire. Varied menu; chicken, veal & seafood. A la carte. Cocktails & lounge. Reservations required. Valet parking. Open 5-11:45 pm. AE, CB, DI, MC, VI. Closed 11/24 & 12/25.

Philips Supper House   *American*   **$$$**   ◆◆◆

(702) 873-5222

2¾ mi w of the Strip, between Arville St & Decatur Blvd at 4545 W Sahara Ave (89102). Prime eastern beef, seafood & Italian specialties. Casual dress. Cocktails & lounge. Reservations suggested. Open 5-11 pm. AE, DI, DS, MC, VI. ⊘

Tony Roma's   *Southwest American*   **$**   ◆

(702) 733-9914

2 mi s on the Strip; 1 mi e on E Sahara Ave at 620 E Sahara Ave (89104). A place for ribs. Children's menu. A la carte. Cocktails & lounge. Open 11 am-10 pm; Fri & Sat to midnight. AE, DI, DS, MC, VI. Closed 12/25. ⊘

Yolie's Brazilian
Steak House   *Ethnic*   **$$**   ◆◆

(702) 794-0700

On upper level of Citibank Park Plaza at 3900 Paradise Rd, Suite Z (89109). Informal atmosphere, variety of meats served from a skewer. Also lamb, chicken & fish specialties; casual dress. A la carte. Children's menu. Cocktails & lounge. Entertainment. Reservations suggested. Open 11:30 am-11 pm; Sat & Sun from 5 pm. AE, CB, DI, MC, VI.

LAUGHLIN

Laughlin is a fascinating phenomenon in the southern Nevada desert. It sits on the west bank of the Colorado River across from Bullhead City, Arizona, 30 miles north of Needles, California. Las Vegas is 100 miles to the north, Los Angeles 285 miles to the southwest. This city by the river attracts about 5 million visitors each year in search of year-round sun where the price is right 24 hours a day.

Before 1966, what is now Laughlin was composed of one roadhouse restaurant. The area was known as South Point, the name of a construction camp that housed workers for nearby Davis Dam. (South Point's population disappeared following completion of the dam in 1953.)

Entrepreneur Don Laughlin purchased and renovated the deteriorating restaurant as a casino in 1966, naming it appropriately "Riverside." Initially, customers for the new business were residents of Bullhead City who were enticed to visit the casino with free ferry service from a parking lot on the Arizona side of the river. As news of the friendly, informal atmosphere of the Riverside Casino got out, people from greater distances showed up. Soon the new business was a great success, and Laughlin expanded his operation. Others quickly saw the potential for

Las Vegas News Bureau

Laughlin has become a boomtown on the banks of the Colorado River.

the gaming business along the shores of the Colorado, and beginning in 1967 with what is now the Golden Nugget (originally called the Bob Cat), additional casino/hotels began to rise. In 1977 the growing community was officially named for its entrepreneur-founder, and today nine major casinos occupy the west riverbank of the Colorado at Laughlin; another sits a block back from the water.

In 1987, Laughlin supplanted Lake Tahoe as Nevada's third-largest gaming resort (after Las Vegas and Reno), and plans for further growth are a major topic of local conversation. Across the river in Bullhead City, the boomtown atmosphere is equally intense.

More than gambling attracts people to the area. The river, with its fishing and water sports, is a major draw, as is the year-round dry, sunny climate. (Laughlin-Bullhead City has become one of America's top destinations for "snowbirds"—escapees from northern winters.)

Rugged mountains provide a scenic backdrop and contain mines and ghost towns of historic importance. Katherine Mine, Chloride and Oatman give travelers an enticing glimpse into the world of the wild west. A drive along historic Route 66 through Oatman and Kingman, Arizona is not only pleasing to the eye, with the area's wonderfully jagged mountaintops, winding roads and alluring vistas, but it serves as a reminder of those who migrated from the parched midwest during the 1930s on this very road, looking for a better life.

Undoubtedly the future will see a dramatic increase in population and development in the Laughlin-Bullhead City area. Already there are plans to build casinos on nearby Indian lands, as well as construct new roads and another bridge across the Colorado River. With the addition of more casinos, tower after tower of hotel rooms, the influx of hundreds of people in the new work force and countless visitors, Laughlin has clearly come a long way from its humble beginnings when coyotes outnumbered the town's population.

TRANSPORTATION

Like the nearby Las Vegas, Laughlin is easily accessible by car, bus or plane. Since the city is quite compact, with most hotels and casinos located within a mile of each other on Casino Row, getting around town is simple: drive, walk, take a taxi or hop on a shuttle or ferry.

TRAVELING TO LAUGHLIN

Air

The Laughlin/Bullhead City Airport is located on SR 95 on the north side of Bullhead City. A new runway has recently been completed so that the airport can accommodate 737s, and a new terminal has opened at the north end of the runway. United Airlines offers direct flights from Los Angeles and connecting service from San Diego.

Auto

The resort town is approximately the same distance from Los Angeles as is Las Vegas, about 5½ hours driving time. The routes from Los Angeles to both Las Vegas and Laughlin begin in a similar manner: I-10 east past Ontario, then north on I-15 to Barstow. At Barstow those bound for Laughlin take I-40 east across the Mojave Desert toward Needles. Approximately 10 miles west of Needles take US 95 north 24 miles, then take SR 163 east about 18 miles to Laughlin Civic Drive. You can choose to drop down into Laughlin or stay on SR 163 and cross over Davis Dam to the Arizona side of the river. Most of SR 163 has been widened to two lanes in each direction, making this a superior route to

either Needles Highway (River Road) or SR 95 on the Arizona side of the river. The one, Needles Highway (River Road), leaves I-40 about four miles west of Needles and travels north to Laughlin on the California-Nevada side of the river. The other, SR 95, travels along the Arizona side of the Colorado—north out of Needles via the Needles Bridge and Harbor Drive to SR 95, then north to Bullhead City, then crosses back over the river to Laughlin via the Laughlin bridge. This second route is more heavily traveled, and severe congestion is frequently encountered at the Laughlin bridge approach. Holiday weekend traffic delays at the bridge can be up to two hours, but the bridge has been widened to four lanes.

Before driving to Laughlin—particularly in the warm-weather months—be sure to read the Desert Driving Hints in the *Las Vegas Transportation* section.

Bus

The routing for bus travelers to the Laughlin/Bullhead City area is through Needles, California, or Las Vegas, Nevada. Greyhound/Trailways offers service from virtually any town in California and Nevada to these cities. From there both Greyhound/Trailways and KT Services bus lines provide daily service to Laughlin. Greyhound/Trailways buses depart the Las Vegas terminal, located at Main Street and Carson Avenue, at 2:10 p.m. and 12:10 a.m. KT Services buses depart the Greyhound/Trailways Terminal at 7 a.m., 11:30 a.m. and 7 p.m. Travel time is 2½ hours. Returning from Laughlin, Greyhound/Trailways departures are at 2:10 and 10:35 p.m. KT Services departs at 2:40 a.m., 1:40 p.m. and 7:25 p.m. In Laughlin the Greyhound/Trailways terminal is at the Riverside Casino entrance; Bullhead City's terminal is at the Bell gas station near 7th and Main streets. Check with a local Greyhound/Trailways agent for ticket and schedule information.

Rental Cars

Auto Club Travel Agency offices and the Airline Express Desk can also help you secure a rental car reservation in advance of your trip. Rental cars are available on a daily or weekly basis from nationally known and local car-leasing agencies. All agencies are based in Bullhead City, most at the airport. Check the telephone directory yellow pages under "Automobile Renting and Leasing." The Hertz rental car agency offers a discount to AAA members at participating locations; call (800) 654-3080.

LOCAL TRANSPORTATION

Shuttles and Ferries

The Riverside, Edgewater, Colorado Belle, Golden Nugget, Pioneer and Gold River hotels in Laughlin have large on-site parking lots, as well as expansive parking areas on the Arizona (Bullhead City) side of the Colorado River with 24-hour **passenger ferry service** across to the casino boat docks. Occasionally the water level of the river (controlled by Davis Dam) is too low for the ferries to travel safely, so parking lot pickups are made by shuttle buses.

Laughlin Transit, Inc. operates several **shuttle** routes in the Laughlin/ Bullhead City area. Exact change is required, and all shuttles operate 24 hours, seven days a week. For route or schedule information call (702) 298-2683; (602) 763-7070, ext. 683; (800) 528-7868.

Route A—Serves the casinos along Casino Drive in Laughlin. Buses depart approximately every 30 minutes, and the fare is $1.35. No transfers.

Route B—Serves the residential areas of Laughlin. Buses leave from the Riverside Resort and travel south on Casino Drive, west on Edison Way and Desert Road to Needles Highway, then south to the communities of El Mirage, Rio Vista, Port Fino, Crown Point, South Point Market, Laughlin Bay Village, Laughlin Estates, and then return. Buses depart hourly, and the fare is $2 (local fare 50¢ for Needles Highway portion). No transfers.

Orange Route—Serves the Casino Drive portion of Laughlin from Harrah's Laughlin Hotel and Casino north to the Laughlin/Bullhead City bridge. The buses then cross the bridge and travel south on SR 95 through Bullhead City, Holiday Shores, Colorado River Estates, Rainbow Acres, Mohave Mesa and Pebble Lake (Chaparral Road), and then return. Buses depart hourly, and the fare is $1.75 within the city limits of Bullhead City; $2.25 to areas out on the mesa (outside the city limits). Transfer to the Green Route is possible.

Green Route—Serves the Holiday Shores, River Bend, Riviera, Riverview Park and Colorado River Estates residential areas on the south side of Bullhead City. Buses depart hourly, and the fare is $1.75. Transfer to the Orange Route is possible.

Taxi

Laughlin has two taxi companies. Bullhead City has four, but the Arizona-based taxi companies are not allowed to operate in Nevada unless called to take a passenger from Laughlin into the state of Arizona; they are not allowed to take passengers from one casino to another or from one location in Nevada to another.

The Laughlin taxi company charges a $2.20 base fare for the first one-seventh mile and 20¢ for each additional one-seventh mile ($1.40 per mile). There is a 20¢ charge for every extra passenger after the first three. Cabs operating in Bullhead City charge $2.20 for the first one-sixth mile and $1.20 for each additional mile.

Laughlin

Desert ....(702) 298-7575
Lucky ....(702) 298-2299

Bullhead City

Checker...............(602) 754-4444
Desert ....(602) 763-0365
Lucky ....(602) 754-1100
                      (602) 763-7200
Yellow ....(602) 754-1111

Sunbathers enjoy the ocean-style beach at Harrah's Laughlin.

CASINO GAMES

Visitors are most often drawn to the Laughlin area for gambling. Slots, live table games and keno lounges take up hundreds of thousands of square feet of casino space. The profits are enormous and have played a major role in fueling the growth of the community.

Las Vegas News Bureau

Slot machines are popular with Laughlin gamblers.

There are currently 10 casinos, with others being planned for the near future. All the casinos offer keno, slot play and 21, and all but the Regency offer craps and roulette. Patrons can find poker tables at the Colorado Belle, Edgewater, Flamingo Hilton, Gold River, Harrah's Laughlin, Ramada Express and Riverside casinos, and bingo at Gold River and the Riverside. Race and sports books are found at the Edgewater, Colorado

Belle, Flamingo Hilton, Gold River and Harrah's Laughlin.

If you are inclined toward trying a game of chance, be sure to familiarize yourself with the rules and strategy of the game. If the game is completely new to you, watch the action for a while before betting. The casinos do occasionally offer lessons in how to play some of the games, but the schedule is sporadic; check with casino management to see if any classes have been scheduled. And finally, decide how much you can afford to lose and set the money aside as your bank. Should you lose it, don't dig into your pockets for more money—it is not just a cliché that people can lose everything they own. See the *Casino Games* section under Las Vegas for a description of each game.

ENTERTAINMENT

Showrooms, lounges and cabarets fill Laughlin resorts with music and song. A variety of entertainment, from well-known singers and comedians to colorful production shows can be found in the various hotel showrooms along Casino Row.

L ounge entertainment is available at all of the Laughlin casinos, although some casinos only offer lounge shows Tuesday through Sunday. The Riverside's Starview Room features a Sunday tea dance from 2 to 6 p.m. every Sunday; no reservations are needed. Also at the Riverside, the Western Dance Hall provides live country music and dancing; call for hours (702) 298-2535, ext. 616; (800) 227-3849.

Main showrooms are listed below. Please note that prices given are per-person minimums and usually do not include sales tax, entertainment tax or any gratuities. In addition to these extra charges, minimums may often be raised for the more popular entertainers or groups. When attending a show, especially one with open seating, remember that the time given is performance time. You should arrive early to secure a good seat. Schedules can change without notice, so you are advised to verify the show, time and price in advance.

Best Western Riverside Resort, 1650 S. Casino Dr. (702) 298-2535, ext. 616; (800) 227-3849
   Don's Celebrity Theatre —Top-name entertainment
      932 seats
      One or two shows nightly; Thursday through Saturday
      VIP and regular seating; prices vary, $15-$30
      Reservations required
      Tickets also sold through Ticketmaster

Flamingo Hilton Laughlin, 1900 S. Casino Dr. (702) 298-5111, (800) 626-2365
   Club Flamingo —"American Superstars" (Indefinitely)
      400 seats
      Sunday through Wednesday and Friday at 8 and 10 p.m.
      Saturday at 6, 8 and 10 p.m.
      Sunday through Wednesday and Friday, $12.95, Saturday $14.95
      Children under 12, $5.95
      Dark Thursday

Amphitheatre—Top-name entertainment
2100 seats outdoors
Prices vary, $12.50-$22.50

Gold River Resort and Casino, 2700 S. Casino Dr. (702) 298-2242, (800) 835-7904
Palace Theatre — Top-name entertainment
400 seats
One show nightly, call for hours
Prices vary with entertainers

SPORTS AND RECREATION

Near perfect weather and the area's natural wonders make Laughlin a year-round playground for outdoor enthusiasts. Recreational opportunities include golf, tennis and a myriad of watersports activities. For those seeking quieter pursuits, many resorts also offer swimming pools, spas and whirlpools for their guests. For a list of facilities at each hotel, see Lodging in this section.

BOATING

Visitors will find the Auto Club's *Guide to Colorado River* to be a useful recreation map of the area. This map should not, however, be used for navigation purposes. Members can obtain this publication at all Auto Club district offices in California and Nevada. Non-members should check with a local bookseller.

Houseboating

Houseboats are permitted on the 75-mile stretch of the Colorado River from Davis Dam south to Parker Dam and north of Davis Dam on Lake Mohave. The Colorado River section from Davis Dam south has varied scenery including rugged mountains, marshes, a narrow canyon (south of Needles) and the wide expanse of Lake Havasu. Boating on Lake Mohave offers numerous coves and inlets to explore in the south part of the lake and the sheer walls of Black Canyon to the far north. The mild winter weather and hot summer days make houseboating popular all year; however, summer thunderstorms are common. Reservations should be made well in advance.

Colorado River
Havasu Springs Resort
Route 2, Box 624
Parker, AZ 85344
(602) 667-3361

Lake Mohave
Cottonwood Cove Resort and Marina
P.O. Box 1000
Cottonwood Cove Road
Cottonwood Cove, NV 89046
(702) 297-1005

Lake Mohave Resort and Marina
Katherine Landing
Bullhead City, AZ 86430
(800) 752-9669, (602) 754-3245

Willow Beach Resort and Marina
Willow Beach Road
Willow Beach, AZ 86445
(800) 845-3833

FISHING

A valid Arizona **fishing license** with a Nevada-Colorado River stamp or a valid Nevada fishing license with an Arizona-Colorado River stamp is required for anyone fishing from a boat or other floating device on Lake Mohave or along the Colorado River section that forms the mutual boundary between Nevada and Arizona. Persons fishing from the shore in Nevada can use either a valid Nevada license, or a valid Arizona license with a Nevada-Colorado River stamp; those fishing from the shore in Arizona can use either a valid Arizona license, or a valid Nevada license with an Arizona-Colorado River stamp. Similar rules apply for the section of the river forming the state boundary for Arizona and California. Fishing licenses can be purchased at bait and tackle shops in Bullhead City. No fishing is allowed in posted areas.

Fishing from shore on an Indian Reservation requires an annual fishing permit. Check with local bait and tackle stores for directions on how to obtain the permit.

There is currently a multi-agency effort underway to protect endangered species of the Colorado River. Fishermen should identify and immediately release humpback chubs, bonytail chubs, razorback suckers and Colorado squawfish that they hook. If you are unfamiliar with these species, they are described in the California and Arizona fishing regulations booklets that are available where licenses are sold.

Colorado River

Fishing is excellent along the Colorado River near the Laughlin-Bullhead City area. **Striped bass** are a popular game fish, and they often tip the scales around 30 pounds. The largest striper ever caught in an inland habitat was landed at Bullhead City and weighed in at 59 pounds, 12 ounces. These fish winter at Lake Havasu and start moving north in the spring, hitting the Laughlin-Bullhead City area in May; common baits are shad, frozen anchovies or sardines with sinkers to keep the bait below the surface of the water. The Striper Derby is held from Memorial Day through Labor Day along the river from Davis Dam

south to Needles; anglers can register at bait and tackle shops in Bullhead City.

Rainbow trout inhabit the cold water along the gravel beds below Davis Dam (no fishing in posted areas). They are also planted south of Laughlin-Bullhead City near the California-Nevada state line from October to June. In warm weather the fish are attracted to lures such as Super Dupers, Panther Martins, spinners and spoons; in cooler weather the best bet is live bait, mostly night crawlers and marshmallow combos. The fish stay in deep water during the day and move toward shore at night. Anglers can also fill their creels with good-sized catfish and largemouth bass, and plenty of bluegill and crappie. **Bass** prefer the cooler deep water and will hit on live bait or floating lures. **Catfish** like stink baits (garlic cheese), dough balls, anchovies and night crawlers. **Bluegill** and **crappie** hit on almost anything that moves—try worms for bluegill and minnows or mini-jigs for crappie.

Lake Mojave

Lake Mohave is noted for its rainbow trout and bass fishing. Trout spend the summer north of Willow Beach and migrate south from October through January. A fish hatchery at Willow Beach provides trout for planting in the lake. Most of the rainbows caught tip the scales near five pounds, some as high as 15. Largemouth bass prefer the deep water at the south end of the lake and only move into shallow water to spawn; trolling live bait at depths of 10 to 30 feet works well to lure them; fishing the coves with floating minnow-shaped lures also works well during the midday hours. Striped bass became established in

1982 when there were high-water releases from Hoover Dam. Striped bass up to three feet are now being caught in Lake Mohave. July and August are the best months for finding catfish in the lake's small coves and inlets. February through April is crappie season; mini-jigs, worms and minnows are the ticket for them.

GOLF

Information given for each course includes name, location, mailing address, phone number and facilities, plus yardage, par and slope and USGA ratings (all from men's white tees). Some 9-hole courses show a slope and USGA rating that reflects play on that 9 holes plus another 9-hole course, or double play on the same course. Unless otherwise stated, each course in open daily all year. The abbreviation N/A means the information was not available. Package plan indicates a special rate combining hotel or resort rooms and golfing fees. Greens fees are given for weekday and weekend play during peak season. Many 9-hole courses list 18-hole fees because they require 18 holes of play. Some courses have senior citizen rates.

Chaparral Country Club (Public)
(602) 758-6330
6 mi s of Bullhead City/Laughlin airport at 1260 E Mohave Dr, 86442. The course is 9 holes; 2306 yards; par 32; 91 slope; 60.6 rating. Rates: $12 weekdays and weekends. Clubhouse, golf shop, power and hand carts, rental clubs, coffee shop, snack bar, beer, wine.

Desert Lakes Golf Club (Public)
(602) 768-1000
13 mi s of Bullhead City/Laughlin bridge via SR 95, left on Joy Ln at 5835 Desert Lakes Dr, 86430.

The course is 18 holes; 6267 yards; par 72; 110 slope; 68.5 rating. Rates: winter $35 (includes golf cart); summer $25 (includes golf cart). Clubhouse, golf shop, professional, power and hand carts, rental clubs, driving range, coffee shop, beer, wine.

Emerald River Golf Course (Public)
(702) 298-0061
3½ mi s of casino center at 1155 W Casino Dr, 89029. Package plan. The course is 18 holes; 5918 yards; par 72; 131 slope; 69.1 rating. Rates: $29 (mandatory golf cart included) weekdays and Sun; $35 (mandatory golf cart included) Sat. Clubhouse, power carts, rental clubs, driving range; snack bar, beer, wine.

Riverview Golf Course (Public)
(602) 763-1818
2¾ mi s on SR 95, 1¼ mi e at Riverview RV Resort, 2000 E Ramar Rd, 86442. The course is 9 holes; 1160 yards; par 27; N/A rating. Rates: $12 for 9 holes, $15 for 18 holes. Clubhouse, golf shop, professional, hand carts, rental clubs, tennis courts, swimming pool, snack bar/deli.

INNER TUBING

Inner tubing is a popular sport along the river. For easy pickup and parking, swimmers usually launch their inner tubes from Davis Camp County Park north of Bullhead City on SR 95, float four or five miles south along the river and disembark at Bullhead Community Park.

SWIMMING

Swimming in the Colorado River is not recommended except from designated beach areas. Public beaches are located at Davis Camp County Park on the Arizona side of the river (north of Bullhead City on SR 95) and at Sportsman's Park on the Nevada

Visitors to the beach at Harrah's Laughlin are treated to views of passing riverboats.

side of the river (north of Laughlin at the junction of Casino Drive and SR 163 at the foot of Davis Dam).

The Pioneer and Harrah's Laughlin hotels also have beach areas, but they are open to hotel guests only. The Del Rio Beach Club at Harrah's Laughlin rents personal watercraft, boats and beach floats.

NOTE: A word of caution to river swimmers south of Davis Dam—the water released from the dam is very cold, about 60 degrees. The best swimming in the area is at Lake Mohave. In the summer the lake water can get as warm as 80 degrees. The beach at Katherine Landing has been closed, but a new beach is in the planning stages, and it should be open by the end of 1994.

Many of the hotels and motels in the area have pools for their guests. For information check the listings under *Lodging.*

TENNIS

The Pioneer Hotel has a tennis court, the Flamingo Hilton has three lighted courts and the Riverview RV Resort in Bullhead City has two lighted courts. These facilities are available to guests only. The events listed are held in Bullhead City unless otherwise stated.

WATERSKIING

Waterskiing is permitted along the Colorado River from Bullhead City south to Needles. A sparsely populated area just south of Bullhead City is usually the best choice for the river. Waterskiing is also permitted on Lake Mohave below mile marker 42. Lake Mohave Resort rents boats and equipment.

ANNUAL EVENTS

Throughout the year Laughlin hotel casinos host a variety of tournaments in 21, poker, craps and slot play. Anyone interested in these tournaments should contact the hotel directly for dates and play information; room reservations should be made well in advance, as room space is often at a premium during a tournament.

One of the highlights of the summer along this stretch of the Colorado River is the Striper Derby, a striped-bass fishing tournament held from May 1 through September 10. There is a $3 entry fee, and a valid fishing license for the area fished is required. The boundaries on the Colorado River for the tournament are from I-40 (near Needles) north to Davis Dam (north of Laughlin). Anglers interested in entering the tournament can register at bait and tackle shops in Bullhead City. Incidentally, the largest striped bass ever caught in an inland freshwater habitat was hooked at Bullhead City; the fish weighed in at 59 pounds, 12 ounces (see Fishing under *Sports and Recreation*).

In addition to entertainment at local casinos, Laughlin and adjacent Bullhead City have a number of annual community events on their calendars. For more information contact the Laughlin Chamber of Commerce at (800) 227-5245 or (702) 298-2214, the Bullhead City Chamber of Commerce at (602) 754-4121, or the Oatman Chamber of Commerce at (602) 768-7400.

January—
Bed Race (Oatman).

February—
Sweetheart Cake Walk (Oatman).

March—
Silvery Colorado Rock Club Gemboree; St. Patrick's Day Party for Jerry's Kids (Oatman).

April—
Desert Twirlers Annual Jamboree; Bullhead City-Laughlin Chili Cook-off; Lake Mohave Boat Show (Katherine Landing); Route 66 Association Road Rally (Oatman).

May—
Veterans of Foreign Wars Parade; Burro Barbecue; Jim Hicklin Air Rallye; Laughlin River Days (Laughlin).

July—
Fireworks display; Sidewalk Egg Fry Challenge (Oatman).

September—
Gold Camp Days (Oatman).

November—
Western Craft Fair; Gold Wing Motorcycle Day (Oatman); Community Christmas Lighting (Oatman).

December—
Christmas Boat Parade of Lights (Katherine Landing to Davis Dam).

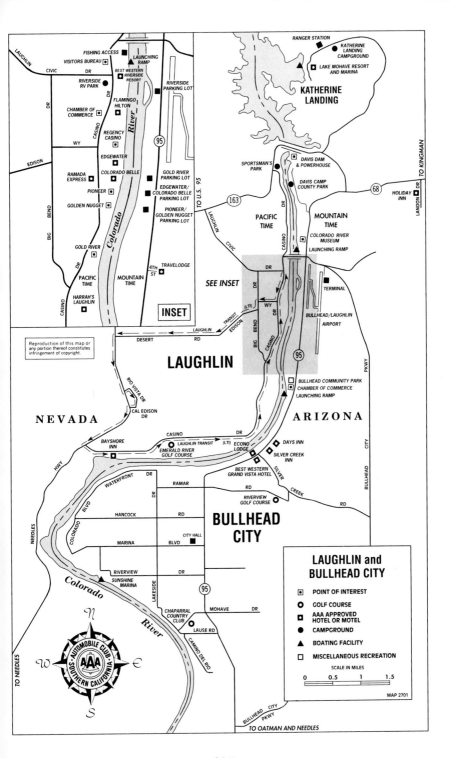

LAUGHLIN and BULLHEAD CITY

POINTS OF INTEREST

Laughlin offers a wide variety of attractions, from museums and guided tours to Old West mining towns. Visitors can while away the hours exploring old Route 66 or taking scenic hikes in nearby recreational areas. Whatever the pleasure, Laughlin's diversity is sure to satisfy most appetites.

COLORADO RIVER MUSEUM, *on the Arizona side of the river, on SR 95 just north of the Laughlin/Bullhead City bridge. (602) 754-3399.* Housed in a historical building that was originally a Catholic church built in 1947 during the Davis Dam construction, this museum features a model of Fort Mohave in the late 1800s, geologic maps of the area, and historical artifacts and photographs. Some of the items donated to the museum include an anchor from one of the steamboats that traveled up and down the Colorado River, mining tools, American Indian artifacts and a piano that was brought around Cape Horn by ship 130 years ago. Hours are Tuesday through Saturday, 10 a.m. to 3 p.m. Donation.

Las Vegas News Bureau

Tourists and residents enjoy a cooling and entertaining commute between casinos on river boat shuttles. Most casinos fronting on the Colorado River have docks and aquatic shuttles.

DAVIS CAMP COUNTY PARK,
on the Arizona side of the river, on SR 95 just north of the Laughlin/Bullhead City bridge. (602) 754-4606. The park offers a stretch of sandy beach for swimming, fishing or launching jet skis, inner tubes, rafts or rubber boats. The area from the park north to Davis Dam is noted for its excellent striped bass and rainbow trout fishing. Visitors have found that a hike into the park's south section can provide views of a variety of birds and small wildlife that populate the marshy area of the park. Camping is permitted in an RV park and along the river (see *Camping*), fishing requires a license (see Fishing, under *Sports and Recreation*), and a boat launching ramp is available. Day use $3. The park is open 24 hours; day use ends at 8 p.m.

DAVIS DAM,
2 miles north of Laughlin via Casino Drive and SR 163. (602) 754-3628. The dam, designed to help regulate the delivery of water to the lower Colorado River region and Mexico, is a rock-fill and earthen structure augmented by concrete intakes and spillways. In addition to its importance for flood control, the dam provides hydroelectric power for regional industry and irrigation for farming. The powerhouse is on the Arizona side of the river and is open for free self-guided tours daily from 7:30 a.m. to 3:30 p.m. (Arizona time). The tours include map displays, a short recorded lecture and a closeup view of major features of the plant.

LAKE MOHAVE
extends 67 miles north from Davis Dam along the Colorado River. Lake Mohave is part of the Lake Mead National Recreation

Davis Dam spans the Colorado River near Laughlin.

Area and is administered by the National Park Service. Ranger stations can be found at the three major recreation areas on the lake: **Katherine Landing,** 6 miles north of Bullhead City via SR 95, SR 68 and north on an unnamed road, (602) 754-3272; **Cottonwood Cove,** 54 miles north of Laughlin via Laughlin Cutoff Road, SR 163, US 95 and an unnamed road east from Searchlight, (702) 297-1229; and **Willow Beach,** 81 miles north of Bullhead City via SR 95, SR 68 to Kingman, US 93 north and an unnamed road west, (602) 767-3340. For more information on Lake Mead see *Points of Interest* under Las Vegas.

Lake Mohave's deep, blue water provides a sharp contrast to the desert landscape surrounding it. Its northern section is almost as narrow as the Colorado River itself, with Indian petroglyphs etched on the steep walls of Black Canyon. The midsection widens to almost four miles before narrowing again in the south, where the shore is lined with hundreds of small coves and inlets.

The contrast of the water to the desert is also reflected in the colorful flora and fauna. The desert provides a home for Gila monsters, scorpions, tarantulas, burros and coyotes; the lake attracts small beavers, muskrats and big horn sheep. There are some 60 species of mammals in the area. Birds run the gamut from hawks and large crows to roadrunners and blue heron. Spring often brings a display of wildflowers (most notably brittlebush and sand verbena) among the desert plants.

Lake Mohave is ideal for boating year round, but those pursuing land adventures will find the best months to visit are October through April. Winters are mild with daytime temperatures generally ranging from 65 to 85 degrees; summer temperatures routinely are at the 100-degree mark and sometimes reach 120.

The lake's main appeal to visitors is in the variety of recreation it offers. Houseboating and fishing are popular pastimes, as are swimming, scuba diving, waterskiing, wind surfing, jet skiing and sunbathing. For information about raft trips in Black Canyon see Lake Mead under Las Vegas *Points of Interest.*

A **fish hatchery** at Willow Beach supplies the rainbow trout that are planted in the lake. The lake has a reputation as one of the best trout and largemouth bass fishing areas in the Southwest (see Fishing, under *Sports and Recreation*).

Houseboats are rented at all three marinas on the lake, but reservations must be made well in advance. (For information on houseboating, see *Sports and Recreation*.)

For map coverage of this area see the Auto Club's *Guide to Colorado River;* this map features boating and camping information, but it should not be used for navigational purposes. These publications are available to members at any Auto Club district office in California or Nevada.

Grapevine Canyon, an area within the Lake Mead National Recreation Area that contains several different ages of American Indian petroglyphs, can be reached by traveling about seven miles west of Davis Dam on SR 163 (approximately six miles west of Casino Drive) and turning north on an unnamed dirt road (a small sign indicates the turn). About two miles along the dirt road is a sign pointing west to a parking area. From the parking area a path leads ½ mile along the edge of a wash and then drops down a small incline into the canyon. Visible at the entrance to the canyon and along the canyon walls are American Indian carvings of animals, fertility symbols and spiritual signs that vary in age from 150 years old to more than 600 years old. The area offers excellent photo opportunities of the petroglyphs. Rangers lead hikes into the canyon twice weekly, and they are hoping to develop several other trails for hiking in the area. Primitive restrooms are available at the parking lot, but hikers must bring their own drinking water. For hiking information call the Katherine Landing ranger station at (602) 754-3272.

Heading north from the Grapevine Canyon parking lot entrance leads to **Christmas Tree Pass** and on to US 95. After about four miles the wide graded dirt road narrows considerably to allow access for only one car in each direction. For about five miles the road is not only narrow, but soft and sandy in places. This section is not recommended for RVs or anyone pulling a trailer. In this section local residents have continued a tradition of decorating the Juniper trees with ribbons, plastic lids, paper and other bits of "trash." As the road leaves this area it widens out again for another five miles to US 95. **NOTE:** This road is subject to heavy washout during periods of rain.

Four-wheel-drive enthusiasts will find several backcountry roads that the National Park Service has approved for public access. They lead to secluded coves on the lake or into the desert mountain backcountry. It is advisable to check with the ranger for information about the road's condition. Flash flooding can occur during inclement weather and sudden summer thunderstorms. Watch for unfenced mine shafts and pits. Stay out of abandoned mines; deep shafts, rotten timbers, and flammable or poisonous gases can be concealed inside the tunnels.

OATMAN, *23 miles southeast of Bullhead City via SR 95 and Boundary Cone Road. (602) 768-7400.* Oatman was a prosperous gold-mining town from 1906 to when the gold ran out in the 1930s; about $36 million worth of ore was taken from local mines. The town has experienced many boom and bust cycles, but being on "Route 66" (US 66) in the 1930s preserved it. (It was the last stop before crossing the Mojave Desert into California.) Today the picturesque ghost town has a population of 100 (200 in winter) and features antique and craft shops, staged gunfights on weekends and a reception committee of wild burros that roam the streets, greeting tourists in hopes of receiving a handout. The Old Gun Shop has a display of guns from the 1820s to 1890s, and the Oatman Jail Museum is open daily from 10 a.m. to 4 p.m. Gunfights are staged Saturday, Sunday and holidays at 2:30 and 4:30 p.m. Some of the saloons feature live entertainment. Bags of alfalfa pellets to feed the burros are sold in local stores.

GOLDROAD, *3 miles northeast of Oatman on SR 66.* All that is left of this gold camp are the foundations of several buildings and an abandoned mine entrance (now closed).

Caution: When exploring near these areas, a four-wheel-drive vehicle is recommended for travel on unpaved roads. Flash flooding can occur during summer thunderstorms, and heavy rains are possible in any season. When exploring old gold camps, watch out for unfenced mine shafts and pits. Never enter abandoned mines; deep shafts, rotted timbers and flammable or poisonous gases can be concealed in the tunnels.

For an interesting **scenic drive** take historic Route 66 (Oatman Highway) north and east out of Oatman to Kingman. The road goes past the abandoned mining camp of Goldroad, climbs to the summit of the Black Mountains and then crosses the wide Sacramento Valley to Kingman. The road climbs from an elevation of 2400 feet in Oatman to 3600 feet at the summit and is at times a series of narrow hairpin curves as it winds its way up to the pass. Those with an adventurous nature will be rewarded with panoramic views of Arizona and Nevada, and maybe even a glimpse of California, on a clear day from the tri-state lookout point just before the summit of Sitgreaves Pass. Then wind down the eastern slope of the Black Mountains into the Sacramento Valley, populated with creosote bushes, yucca plants and occasionally in season, a sprinkling of wildflowers. For the return to the Bullhead City/Laughlin bridge, take SR 68 west from Kingman across the flat Sacramento Valley, descend through a pass at the north end of the Black Mountains and drop down into the Colorado River Valley arriving back at the foot of the bridge. Total mileage (from Oatman) is 60 miles.

NOTE: This trip is not recomended for those travelers with large recreational vehicles or those pulling large trailers.

GUIDED TOURS

Taking a tour is a convenient way to see and learn about an area's attractions. Laughlin offers several such tours, most in the form of nar-rated boat excursions. Seasonal periodic low water levels on the river (controlled by Davis Dam) or weather conditions may affect cruise schedules. Be sure to contact the companies in advance for complete information and reservations.

Tours listed below are for visitors' information and convenience. The Automobile Club of Southern California does not recommend one tour company over another and cannot guarantee the services offered.

LAUGHLIN RIVER TOURS, INC.,
P.O. Box 29279 (89028). (702) 298-1047, (800) 228-9825.

Fiesta Queen Tour—
A one-hour narrated cruise in the Laughlin-Bullhead City area. Departs from Harrah's Laughlin Hotel & Casino boat dock. Six cruises daily, starting at 11:30 a.m., last cruise 6:30 p.m. Adults $10, ages 12 and under $6. 150-passenger sidewheeler with air-conditioned lower deck. Snack and beverage bar. Upper deck provides open-air seating. Live entertainment offered on selected cruises. Ticket booth located at Harrah's Laughlin Hotel & Casino.

Little Belle Tour—
A one-hour narrated cruise in the Laughlin-Bullhead City area. Departs from Edgewater Casino boat dock. Six cruises daily, starting at 11:30 a.m., last cruise 6:30 p.m. Adults $10, ages 12 and under $6. 150-passenger side-wheeler with air conditioned lower deck. Upper deck provides open-air seating. Snack and beverage bar. Dinner cruise available with live entertainment on selected cruises; reservations advised. Ticket booth located on Edge-

water Casino boat dock, (702) 298-2453, ext. 3877.

BLUE RIVER SAFARIS, *P.O. Box 507 (89029). (702) 298-0910, (800) 345-8990.*

London Bridge Tour—An all-day narrated tour which begins by bus to Park Moabi Marina, then by boat through scenic Topock Gorge to Lake Havasu City and then returns by bus with a stop in Oatman. Departs daily from the Colorado Belle Hotel and Casino boat dock. Daily at 9:30 a.m., returning at 5:30 p.m. (Arizona time). $60 per person (includes lunch). Boat docks near London Bridge for lunch and shopping (2 hours). 40-foot jet cruiser holds 48 passengers. Ticket booth located at the Colorado Belle Hotel and Casino, on the back deck overlooking the river.

In December and January, when weather and wind conditions affect river boat travel, Blue River Safaris offers its London Bridge Tour by bus. Tour departs from the Colorado Belle Hotel and Casino. $45 per person (includes lunch).

U.S.S. RIVERSIDE, *Riverside Resort and Casino, P.O. Box 500 (89029). (702) 298-2535, ext. 5770, (800) 227-3849, ext. 5770.*

Davis Dam Tour—
One-hour, 15-minute narrated tour of Laughlin-Bullhead City area including Davis Dam. Departs from the Riverside Casino boat dock. Five cruises daily Monday through Friday, starting at 10:30 a.m., last cruise 6:30 p.m. Cruises begin every two hours. Six cruises on Saturday, starting at 10:30 a.m., last cruise 8:30 p.m. Cruises begin every two hours. Adults $10, children ages 3-12, $6. Luxury cruiser designed to travel under the Laughlin-Bullhead City bridge. Beverage bar available. Upper deck offers open-air seating. Ticket booth located on the ground level of the Riverside Casino, near the door to the boat dock.

Robert Brown

Old Route 66 climbs steeply out of Oatman toward Kingman by way of a number of hairpin curves, but offers spectacular views of the valley below.

ACTIVITIES FOR CHILDREN

While Laughlin's orientation toward gambling is geared mostly to adults, parents will find plenty of activities to entertain their children. Hiking, fishing and swimming are popular pastimes, and exploring the old mining town of Oatman is always a treat for the kids.

*T*he Colorado Belle, Edgewater, Flamingo Hilton, Gold River, Harrah's Laughlin, Ramada Express, Pioneer and Riverside hotels all have video arcade areas. First-run movies are available at the Riverside Resort and in Bullhead City. Boat trips on the river (see

Chris Hart

Friendly engineers and conductors take passengers around the parking lot on a narrow-gauge train at the Ramada Express Hotel.

Points of Interest) offer not only fresh air, but adventure.

The Ramada Express Hotel has an on-site narrow-gauge railroad to the parking lot with a steam locomotive that can be a fun ride for small children. The train consists of an engine and two open-air passenger cars that together have a 65-passenger capacity. The rides are free and the train operates daily. For more information, phone (702) 298-4200. Inside the hotel there is a play area for younger children that also features a train.

If outdoor recreation is a pastime your child enjoys, Davis Camp County Park offers areas for hiking and fishing. (See listing under *Points of Interest.*)

Information on fishing, swimming, inner tubing and waterskiing can be found under *Sports and Recreation.*

A trip to Oatman will be a treat for most children. A group of friendly but wild burros roam the streets, and they often greet visitors in hopes of a handout (alfalfa pellets are sold at local stores). Picking through antique and souvenir shops may turn up some lost "treasure" or a keepsake to take home. Gunfights are staged on weekends and holidays. (See listing under *Points of Interest.*)

Children might also enjoy one of the boat cruises on the Colorado River, a trip to see American Indian petroglyphs at Grapevine Canyon, the Colorado River Historical Museum or a tour of Davis Dam. (See listings under *Points of Interest.*)

Robert Brown

Wild burros roam the streets of picturesque Oatman.

CAMPING

Camping is popular in the Laughlin area, and many campgrounds offer full RV hookups. The following listings are divided into sections: Laughlin and the surrounding areas of Bullhead City, Arizona, and Lake Mohave (Lake Mead National Recreation Area).

The ⒶⒶⒶ preceding a campground indicates the property is a AAA-approved facility and can display the AAA sign. A checkmark (√) after the name of the campground indicates that it is privately owned and has been inspected. County, state and federal campgrounds have not been inspected by AAA, but are listed as a convenience to readers. Those campgrounds listed under **Other** may not meet all AAA standards but are listed as a service.

Each listing contains the total number of sites and the opening and closing dates. Rates quoted represent daily camping fees. Each listing includes the campground's location, mailing address and telephone number (if available), as well as a brief description. Unless otherwise noted, all campgrounds have drinking water, showers and flush toilets and will accept pets on leashes.

Abbreviations are used as follows: (T) indicates number of sites for tent campers; (T/RV) indicates the number of interchangeable tent or recreational vehicle sites; (RV) indicates the number of sites exclusively for recreational vehicles. Electric, water and sewage hookups are designated by E, W and S; these are followed by the number of hookups available and any charges.

Many public campgrounds have limits on the number of consecutive days a visitor may stay. Travelers are advised to check directly with the campground regarding these limitations. Limits are usually as follows:

**Bureau of Land
Management (BLM)**   14 days

**County Parks (County)
District Parks** 14 days to no limit

**National Forests (NF)
State Forests (State)** 5 to 14 days

**National Parks and
Monuments (NPS)** 7, 14 or 30 days

State Parks (State)   14 days

Some private campgrounds have 14-day stay limits for campers renting on a weekly basis. Many have monthly rates and sections of their RV parks that house "long term" residents. The rates and information for campgrounds listed are specifically for "overnight" camping or for campers staying only a few days. For longer visits, arrangements should be made directly with the campground.

Major credit cards honored by the campgrounds are abbreviated as follows: AE=American Express; DI=Diner's Club International; DS=Discover; MC=Mastercard; VI=Visa.

RV towing and tire-change service is available to Auto Club members for motorhomes, campers and travel/camping trailers. Information about these services is available at Auto Club offices.

LAUGHLIN
Public

Sportsman's Park   59 sites   Open all year   Rates Subject to Change
A/Y $6
2 mi n via Casino Dr and SR 163, at the foot of Davis Dam (Box 652, 89029).
T/RV-59. Senior discount. Flush toilets. No showers. Beach; picnic area; boat ramp (free). (County)   (702) 298-3377

Other

The following establishment may not meet all AAA standards but is listed as a service.

Riverside RV Park   800 sites   Open all year   Rates Subject to Change
A/Y $14   EWS-500
Casino Dr and Laughlin Cutoff Rd (Box 500, 89029). RV-800. Flush toilets; hot showers. Pool; boat ramp. Coin laundry. Propane. Restaurant. Casino across road at resort. 14-day stay limit.   (702) 298-2535

BULLHEAD CITY, AZ
Public

Mohave County Parks-
Davis Camp   154 sites   Open all year   Rates Subject to Change
A/Y $8-$15   EW-30, S-124
1 mi n on SR 95, below Davis Dam. 365 acres. RV-130. On Colorado River. Attendant. Hospital in town. Disposal station. Flush & pit toilets. Boating; fishing. Visitor center. Pets, limit 2. 14-day stay limit on beach. MC, VI. (County)   (602) 754-4606

LAKE MOHAVE
Public

Cottonwood Cove   149 sites   Open all year   Rates Subject to Change
A/Y $8   EWS-75
14 mi e of Searchlight on SR 164 (Box 123, Searchlight, 89046). 3 acres. T/RV-149. Hospital in Henderson, 55 miles. Reservations not accepted. Showers. Rental boats. Pets. 30-day stay limit. (NPS)   (702) 297-1229

Katherine Landing   212 sites   Open all year   Rates Subject to Change
A/Y $8   EWS-27
5 mi n of Bullhead City, off SR 68 (c/o 601 Nevada Hwy, Boulder City, NV, 89005). 17 acres. T-173; RV-39. Attendant. Hospital in Bullhead City, 5 mi. Coin laundry; showers; propane; restaurant. Rental boats; boat ramp; fishing; swimming; recreational program. 30-day stay limit. (NPS)   (602) 754-3272

AAA Approved
Private

Cottonwood Cove
RV Park & Marina (√) 73 sites   Open all year   Rates Subject to Change
  Ⓞ A/Y $17   EWS-73
    Between Las Vegas & Needles; 14 mi e of Searchlight, off US 95 on Lake Mohave (89046). In the Lake Mead National Recreation Area; desert landscape. 20 acres; RV-73. Flush toilets. Coin laundry. Beach; swimming; boat ramp; marina; fishing. Groceries; propane. Disposal station. Fee for houseboats, powerboats, waterskiing & equipment. Pets. A/C $3. Credit card guarantee. AE, DS, MC, VI. Lounge, snack bar.   (702) 297-1464

Chris Hart

Katherine Landing, on Lake Mohave, has full marina services in addition to camping facilities.

LODGING AND RESTAURANTS

Wherever one chooses to stay, it is important that reservations be made as far in advance as possible, especially for weekend and holiday periods.

Laughlin draws more than 50,000 visitors to its casinos on an average weekend, and holiday crowds can be even larger. While space is limited in Laughlin, additional lodging can also be found across the river in Bullhead City, Arizona. Passenger ferries provide frequent service from parking lots on the Arizona side of the river to the various casinos on the Nevada side, and 24-hour shuttle bus service is available between the two cities. A reservation deposit is often required; when making reservations, be sure to check with the hotel or motel regarding amount of deposit and refund policy. Auto Club members can make hotel and motel reservations at any Auto Club district office.

Similar to Las Vegas, all the large casino/hotels in Laughlin have several restaurants, some with themed dining rooms overlooking the river, which feature regional or ethnic food.

Also a number of restaurants and major fast-food franchise outlets can be found across the river in Bullhead City. Prices in Laughlin range from a low of about $2 for breakfast to a high of $30 for a gourmet dinner. Buffets are common and range in price from $4 to $6; buffet breakfasts are priced from $2 to $3.50; and lunches are priced similarly. Buffet dinners usually include a choice of two or three entrees, plus potato, vegetable, salad, dessert and beverage. Buffet-style champagne brunches are offered on Sunday. In addition to restaurants and buffets, most of the hotels have coffee shops that are open 24 hours. A list of AAA-approved restaurants follows the hotel and motel listings.

A complete description of lodging and restaurant listings is found beginning on page 71 .

LODGING
LAUGHLIN

Bayshore Inn
(702) 299-9010; FAX (702) 299-9194

		Motel	◆◆
		Rates Subject to Change	
Fri & Sat	1P 55.00	2P/1B 65.00	2P/2B 65.00	XP 7
Sun-Thu	1P 22.00	2P/1B 30.00	2P/2B 30.00	XP 7

7 mi s of Davis Dam at 1955 W Casino Dr (Box 31377, 89029). 105 rooms; central pool deck. 3 stories; interior corridors. Cable TV. Pool; whirlpool. Boat ramp. Fishing. Small pets only, $10. Children 14 & under stay free; senior discount. Credit card guarantee. AE, DS, MC, VI. Cocktails & lounge. Ⓓ Ⓢ ⊘

Best Western Riverside Resort ⓐⓐⓐ Motor Inn ◆◆◆

(702) 298-2535; FAX (702) 298-2614 *Rates Subject to Change*

Fri & Sat	1P 75.00-85.00	2P/1B 75.00-85.00	2P/2B 75.00-85.00	XP 8
Sun-Thu	1P 45.00-59.00	2P/1B 45.00-59.00	2P/2B 45.00-59.00	XP 8

2 mi s of Davis Dam; across river from Bullhead City, AZ; 1650 S Casino Way (Box 500, 89029). 659 rooms. On the Colorado River. 2-14 stories; interior corridors; conference facilities; meeting rooms. Some shower baths; cable TV; pay movies; rental refrigerators; some safes. Fee for whirlpools. 2 pools. Valet parking. No pets. Children 12 & under stay free; senior discount. Reservation deposit required; 3-day refund notice. AE, DI, DS, MC, VI. Dining room; restaurant; 24 hours; $7-$30; cocktails; buffet, $4; casino; name entertainment. Ⓓ Ⓢ ⊘

Colorado Belle Hotel & Casino ⓐⓐⓐ Hotel ◆◆◆

(702) 298-4000; FAX (702) 299-0669 *Rates Subject to Change*

Fri & Sat	1P 49.00-59.00	2P/1B 49.00-59.00	2P/2B 49.00-59.00
Sun-Thu	1P 32.00	2P/1B 32.00	2P/2B 32.00

3 mi s of Davis Dam at 2100 S Casino Dr (Box 2304, 89029). 1238 rooms. On the Colorado River; riverboat design. Suites, 6 with whirlpool bath, $85-$120 for up to 4 persons. 6 stories; interior/exterior corridors. Safes; shower baths; rental refrigerators. 2 pools; whirlpool. Valet parking. No pets. Credit card guarantee. AE, CB, DI, DS, MC, VI. 3 restaurants; coffee shop; 24 hours; $7-$25; cocktails & lounge; buffet. Ⓓ Ⓢ ⊘

Edgewater Hotel ⓐⓐⓐ Hotel ◆◆◆

(702) 298-2453; FAX (702) 298-8165 *Guaranteed Rates*

Fri & Sat	1P 49.00-59.00	2P/1B 49.00-59.00	2P/2B 49.00-59.00
Sun-Thu	1P 23.00-30.00	2P/1B 23.00-30.00	2B/2B 23.00-30.00

3 mi s of Davis Dam at 2020 S Casino Dr (Box 30707, 89028). 1453 rooms. On the Colorado River; some rooms with river view. Maximum rates for up to 4 persons; 3-26 stories; interior corridors. Cable TV; rental refrigerators. Pool; whirlpool. Valet parking. No pets. Credit card guarantee. AE, CB, DI, DS, MC, VI. Dining room; coffee shop; 24 hours; $5-$20; cocktails; buffet, $4. Ⓓ Ⓢ ⊘

Flamingo Hilton–Laughlin ⓐⓐⓐ Hotel ◆◆◆

(702) 298-5111; FAX (702) 298-5177 *Rates Subject to Change*

Fri & Sat	1P 65.00	2P/1B 65.00	2P/2B 65.00	XP 7
Sun-Thu	1P 35.00	2P/1B 35.00	2P/2B 35.00	XP 7

2 mi s of Davis Dam at 1900 S Casino Dr (89029). 1986 rooms; most with view of Colorado River; spacious rooms. 18 stories; interior corridors; conference facilities. Cable TV; pay movies. Pool; 3 lighted tennis courts. Data ports. Valet parking. No pets. Children stay free. Credit card guarantee. AE, DI, DS, MC, VI. 2 restaurants; coffee shop; 24 hours; $9-$21; buffet, $5; casino; cocktails & lounge; entertainment. Ⓓ Ⓢ ⊘

Harrah's Casino Hotel Hotel ◆◆◆

(702) 298-4600; FAX (702) 298-6896 *Rates Subject to Change*

Fri & Sat	1P 55.00-90.00	2P/1B 55.00-90.00	2P/2B 55.00-90.00	XP 7

5 mi s of Davis Dam at 2900 S Casino Dr (Box 33000, 89029). 1658 rooms; on the Colorado River; Southwest architecture. Some shower baths; cable TV; pay movies. Beach; 2 pools; whirlpool. Valet parking. No pets. Reservation deposit required. AE, DI, DS, MC, VI. Dining room; 2 restaurants; coffee shop; 24 hours; $10-$25; buffet, $8; Fri, $13; cocktails; also *William Fisk's Steakhouse*, see separate listing. Entertainment; nightclub. Ⓓ Ⓢ ⊘

Ramada Express Hotel & Casino — Hotel ◆◆◆

(702) 298-4200; FAX (702) 298-4619   *Rates Subject to Change*

Fri & Sat	1P 54.00-59.00	2P/1B 54.00-59.00	2P/2B 54.00-59.00	XP 7
Sun-Thu	1P 23.00-34.00	2P/1B 23.00-34.00	2P/2B 23.00-34.00	XP 7

3 mi s of Davis Dam at 2121 S Casino Dr (Box 77771, 89028). 1500 rooms; railroad motif. 12-23 stories; interior corridors. Shower baths; pay movies. Pool; whirlpool. Train ride. Valet parking. No pets. Children 18 & under stay free. Reservation deposit required. AE, DI, DS, MC, VI. Restaurant; coffee shop; 24 hours; $10-$20; buffet, $4; casino; cocktail lounge. Ⓓ Ⓢ ⊘

SURROUNDING AREAS
BULLHEAD CITY, ARIZONA

Best Western Grand Vista Hotel — Motel ◆◆◆

(602) 763-3300; FAX (602) 763-4447   *Rates Subject to Change*

Fri & Sat	1P 60.00-95.00	2P/1B 60.00-95.00	2P/2B 60.00-95.00
Sun-Thu	1P 48.00-55.00	2P/1B 48.00-55.00	2P/2B 48.00-55.00

2 mi s on SR 95 at 1817 Arcadia Plaza (86442). 80 rooms. Located on a hill with a view of the Colorado River. 3 stories; interior corridors; meeting room. Cable TV; free movies. Some refrigerators. Pool; whirlpool. No pets. Discount for children. Weekly rates available. Reservation deposit required. AE, CB, DI, DS, MC, VI. Restaurant nearby. Ⓓ ⊘

Days Inn ⒶⒶⒶ — Motel ◆◆

(602) 758-1711; FAX (602) 758-7937   *Rates Subject to Change*

Fri & Sat [CP]	1P 45.00	2P/1B 45.00	2P/2B 55.00	XP 5
Sun-Thu [CP]	1P 35.00	2P/1B 35.00	2P/2B 45.00	XP 5

1½ mi s on SR 95, 1 blk e at 2200 Karis Dr (86442). 70 rooms. Formerly First Choice Inn. Located off main highway. Suites, $65-$95 for 2 persons. 3 stories; interior corridors. Cable TV; free movies; rental VCPs; some shower baths; refrigerators. Some efficiencies; utensils; microwaves. Pool; whirlpool. Coin laundry. Small pets only, $50 deposit, $12 non-refundable. Children 12 & under stay free. Senior discount. Weekly & monthly rates available. AE, CB, DI, DS, MC, VI. Ⓓ Ⓢ ⊘

Econo Lodge ⒶⒶⒶ — Motel ◆◆

(602) 758-8080; FAX (602) 758-8283   *Rates Subject to Change*

Fri & Sat [CP]	1P 38.00	2P/1B 44.00	2P/2B 58.00	XP 6
Sun-Thu [CP]	1P 32.00	2P/1B 32.00	2P/2B 45.00	XP 6

2 mi s on SR 95 at 1717 Hwy 95 (86442). 64 rooms; some riverfront units with patio or balcony. Suites, $55-$65. 2 stories; exterior corridors. Some shower baths; cable TV; some refrigerators; microwaves. Small pool. Coin laundry. No pets. Children 12 & under stay free. Senior Discount. Credit card guarantee. AE, DS, MC, VI. Ⓓ Ⓢ ⊘

Holiday Inn–Bullhead City/Laughlin — Motor Inn ◆◆◆

(602) 754-4700; FAX (602) 754-1225   *Rates Subject to Change*

9/1-5/31	1P 45.00	2P/1B 50.00	2P/2B 50.00	XP 5
6/1-8/31	1P 35.00	2P/1B 35.00	2P/2B 35.00	XP 5

3 mi n on SR 95, 1¼ mi e on SR 68E in Sun Ridge Estates at 839 Landon Dr (86430). 155 rooms. Quiet location off highway; landscaped courtyard. 4 stories; exterior corridors; conference rooms; meeting rooms. Cable TV; some shower baths; some refrigerators. Exercise room; heated pool; whirlpool. Airport transportation. Small pets only, $50 deposit required. Weekly rates available. AE, CB, DI, DS, ER, JCB, MC, VI. Restaurant; 6 am-2 pm & 5-9 pm; Fri & Sat to 10 pm; $6-$14; cocktails. Ⓓ Ⓢ ⊘

Lake Mohave Resort ⓐⓐⓐ

Motor Inn ◆

(602) 754-3245; FAX (602) 754-1125

Rates Subject to Change

All Year   1P ...   2P/1B 60.00-69.00 2P/2B 73.00-83.00   XP 6

3 mi n of SR 68 & Davis Dam, at Katherine Landing (86430). 51 rooms. Spacious landscaped grounds. 2 stories; exterior corridors. Some shower baths; cable TV; some efficiencies; utensils. Coin laundry. Beach; swimming; boating; boat ramp; marina; waterskiing; fishing. Fee for houseboats. Small pets only, $10 daily & $25 deposit. Children 12 & under stay free. Senior discount. Credit card guarantee. MC, VI. Restaurant; 8 am-8 pm; Fri & Sat from 7 am; $9-$14; cocktails. Ⓓ

Silver Creek Inn ⓐⓐⓐ

Motor Inn ◆◆◆

(602) 763-8400

Rates Subject to Change

Fri & Sat	1P 54.00	2P/1B 54.00	2P/2B 54.00	XP 5
Sun-Thu	1P 44.00	2P/1B 44.00	2P/2B 44.00	XP 5

1¼ mi s on SR 95 at 1670 Hwy 95 (86442). 68 rooms. 3 stories; interior corridors; large rooms; meeting rooms. Refrigerators; some shower baths; cable TV. Small pool. Small pets only, $50 deposit. Children 11 & under stay free. Weekly rates available. Reservation deposit required. AE, CB, DI, DS, MC, VI. Restaurant; 7 am-2 pm; Sat & Sun from 8 am, closed Mon; $4-$6. Ⓓ

Travelodge ⓐⓐⓐ

Motel ◆◆◆

(602) 754-3000; FAX (602) 754-5234

Rates Subject to Change

Fri & Sat [CP]	1P 55.00-65.00	2P/1B 55.00-65.00	2P/2B 55.00-65.00	XP 5
Sun-Thu [CP]	1P 35.00-45.00	2P/1B 45.00-55.00	2P/2B 45.00-55.00	XP 5

1¼ mi s on SR 95, 1 blk e at 2360 4th St (Box 3037, 86430). 90 rooms; 1 blk off main highway. 2 stories; exterior corridors. Cable TV; free movies; some shower baths; refrigerators; some microwaves. Pool; whirlpool. Pets, $5 daily & $50 deposit required. Senior discount. Weekly rates available. Credit card guarantee. AE, CB, DI, DS, JCB, MC, VI. Ⓓ Ⓢ ⊘

COTTONWOOD COVE, NEVADA

Cottonwood Cove Motel ⓐⓐⓐ

Motel ◆◆

(702) 297-1464; FAX (702) 297-1464

Rates Subject to Change

3/15-10/31	1P 90.00	2P/1B 90.00	2P/2B 85.00	XP 6
11/1-3/14	1P 65.00	2P/1B 65.00	2P/2B 60.00	XP 6

Between Las Vegas & Needles; 14 mi e of Searchlight off US 95 (Box 1000, 89046). 24 rooms. Overlooking Lake Mojave. Exterior corridors. Free movies; cable TV; rental VCPs; some shower baths. Coin laundry. Beach; boat ramp; marina; swimming; fishing; waterskiing; houseboats. Power boats & equipment. No pets. Children 5 & under stay free. Credit card guarantee; 3-day refund notice. AE, DS, MC, VI. Coffee shop; 7 am-8 pm; 9/6-5/27 to 7 pm; $4-$8. Ⓓ ⊘

RESTAURANT
LAUGHLIN

**William Fiske's
Steakhouse**   *American*   **$$$**   ◆◆

(702) 298-6832

In Harrah's Del Rio at 2900 S Casino Dr (89029). Intimate dining atmosphere overlooking Colorado River. A la carte. Varied menu. Cocktails. Reservations suggested. Valet parking. Open 6-10 pm; Fri & Sat to 11 pm. AE, DI, DS, MC, VI.

Rich DePrez, Ace Photography

The Laughlin skyline reflects the community's rapid growth during the past decade.

REFERENCE PHONE NUMBERS FOR LAS VEGAS

Area Code: (702)

Emergency: 911

Nevada Highway Patrol: dial "0" and ask for Zenith 1-2000

California Highway Patrol: dial "0" and ask for Zenith 1-9000

Highway Conditions: (702) 486-3116

AAA Emergency Road Service Numbers:
(800) AAA-HELP
(in the USA and Canada)
(800) 955-4TDD
(for the hearing impaired)

AAA Offices:
California State
Automobile Association
3312 W. Charleston Boulevard
Las Vegas, NV 89102
(702) 870-9171
Office hours: 8:30 a.m. to 5 p.m.
Monday through Friday

California State
Automobile Association
601 Whitney Ranch Drive, #A
Henderson, NV 89014
(702) 458-2323
Office hours: 8:30 a.m. to 5 p.m.
Monday through Friday

Time: 118

Weather:
(702) 734-2010 (Las Vegas)
(702) 736-3854
(Mt. Charleston, Lake Mead)

REFERENCE PHONE NUMBERS FOR LAUGHLIN

Area Codes:	Laughlin (702) Bullhead City (602)
Emergency:	Dial "0"
Fire and Medical Emergency:	(800) 772-7282
Nevada Highway Patrol:	Dial "0" and ask for Zenith 1-2000
California Highway Patrol:	(619) 326-2000
Nevada Highway Conditions:	(702) 486-3116
AAA Emergency Road Service:	(800) AAA-HELP (in the USA and Canada) (800) 955-4TDD (for the hearing impaired)
Nearest AAA Offices:	California State Automobile Association 601 Whitney Ranch Drive, #A Henderson, NV 89014 (702) 458-2323 Office hours: 8:30 a.m. to 5 p.m. Monday through Friday California State Automobile Association 3312 W. Charleston Boulevard Las Vegas, NV 89102 (702) 870-9171 Office hours: 8:30 a.m. to 5 p.m. Monday through Friday
Time and Temperature:	(602) 763-3000 (Bullhead City)

Remember when crossing back and forth from Laughlin, Nevada, to Bullhead City, Arizona, that you are crossing from one time zone (Pacific Time) to another (Mountain Time). During Standard Time periods from late October through early April, Arizona is one hour ahead of Nevada; during the rest of the year the time is the same in both cities.

INDEX TO POINTS OF INTEREST

Alan Bible Visitor Center..........49
Artemus W. Ham
    Concert Hall 46

Black Canyon Raft Trips...........51
Boulevard Mall 28
Buccaneer Bay/Mutiny Bay.......39
Bureau of Land Management
    Visitor Center.......................51

Cactus Gardens (Ethel M
    Chocolates Factory) 47
Cashman Field Center..............39
Cathedral Rock.........................54
Charleston Peak 54
Christmas Tree Pass................111
Clark County Museum..............47
Colorado River Cruises
    (Laughlin)............................112
Colorado River Museum.........108

Davis Camp County Park 109
Davis Dam................................109
Davis Dam Tour 113
Debbie Reynolds' Hollywood
    Museum................................39
Deer Creek 54
Donna Beam Fine Art Gallery ...46
Downtown Trolley
    (Las Vegas) 14

Ethel M Chocolates Factory......47

Fashion Show Mall 28
Fiesta Queen Tour...................112
Flashlight 46
Floyd Lamb State Park 47
Forum Shops at Caesars...........29

Goldroad 111
Grand Canyon Flights 56
Grand Slam Canyon 39
Grapevine Canyon...................110
Guinness World of Records
    Museum and Gift Shop..........40

Hoover Dam 48
Hoover Dam Guided Tours 48

Imperial Palace Auto
    Collection..............................41

Judy Bayley Theatre 46

Kidd's Marshmallow Factory....48

Lake Mead Boat Cruises 50
Lake Mead Fish Hatchery 51
Lake Mead Guided Tours 56
Lake Mead National
    Recreation Area....................48
Lake Mohave 109
Lake Mohave Raft Trips 51
Las Vegas Art Museum 41
Las Vegas Convention
    Center 41
Las Vegas Factory Stores..........29
Las Vegas Guided Tours...........56
Las Vegas Museum of
    Natural History 41
Las Vegas Speedway 41
Lee Canyon Ski Area 54
Liberace Museum 41
Lied Discovery Children's
    Museum................................42
Little Belle Tour 112
London Bridge Tour...............113

Lost City Museum 51
Luxor Entertainment
    Complex...............................43

Marjorie Barrick Museum of
    Natural History 46
Meadows Mall...........................29
MGM Grand Adventures...........43
Museum of Natural History
    (Las Vegas Museum of Natural
    History)................................41
Museum of Natural History
    (UNLV) 46

Nellis Air Force Base 44
Nevada State Museum and
    Historical Society..................44
North Shore Road.....................50

Oatman 111
Old Las Vegas Mormon
    Fort State Park......................39
Old Mill 54
Omnimax® Theatre 44

Passenger Ferry (Laughlin).......95
Red Rock Canyon National
    Conservation Area.................51

Sam Boyd Silver Bowl..............46
Scandia Family Fun Center 45
Scenic Loop Drive 53
Shuttle Service (Laughlin) 95
Southern Nevada Zoological
    Park......................................45
Spring Mountain Ranch State
    Park......................................53
Stratosphere Tower..................45
Strip Trolley (Las Vegas) 14

Thomas and Mack Center 46
Thunderbird Museum 44
Toiyabe National Forest 53

University of Nevada
    Las Vegas 45

Valley of Fire State Park 54

Wet 'N Wild 46

INDEX TO ADVERTISERS

Adventure Airlines ....Las Vegas 57
Center Strip Inn.........................Las Vegas.................Inside Front Cover
Eagle Canyon Airlines................Las Vegas 58
Flamingo Hilton ....Las Vegas 82
Las Vegas Wedding
    Coordinators ....Las Vegas 30
Primadonna Resort & Casino.........Jean 89
Sam's Town Hotel ....Las Vegas 87
Wet N' Wild ....Las Vegas 47

For information about placing an advertisement in Automobile Club of Southern California publications, please contact

Ginger Nichols or Karen Clyne
Advertising Services H076
Auto Club of Southern California
P.O. Box 2890
Los Angeles, CA 90051
(213) 741-3571